# 200 *Fa*
## one pot meals

# 200 *Fast*
## one pot meals
hamlyn **all color**

An Hachette UK Company
www.hachette.co.uk

First published in Great Britain in 2015 by Hamlyn a division
of Octopus Publishing Group Ltd, Endeavour House,
189 Shaftesbury Avenue, London, WC2H 8JY
www.octopusbooks.co.uk
www.octopusbooksusa.com

Copyright © Octopus Publishing Group Ltd 2015

Distributed in the US by Hachette Book Group
1290 Avenue of the Americas, 4th and 5th Floors,
New York, NY 10020

Distributed in Canada by Canadian Manda Group,
664 Annette St., Toronto, Ontario, Canada  M6S 2C8

Some of the recipes in this book have previously appeared
in other titles published by Hamlyn.

ISBN 13: 978-0-600-63089-0

Printed and bound in China

1 2 3 4 5 6 7 8 9 10

Standard level kitchen cup and spoon measurements
are used in all recipes.

Ovens should be preheated to the specified temperature;
if using a convection oven, follow the manufacturer's
instructions for adjusting the time and temperature.

Fresh herbs should be used unless otherwise stated.

Eggs should be large unless otherwise stated. The
U.S. Food And Drug Administration advises that eggs
should not be consumed raw. This book contains dishes
made with raw or lightly cooked eggs. It is prudent for more
vulnerable people, such as pregnant and nursing mothers,
people with weakened immune systems, the elderly, babies,
and young children, to avoid uncooked or lightly cooked
dishes made with eggs. Once prepared, these dishes
should be kept refrigerated and used promptly.

This book includes dishes made with nuts and
nut derivatives. It is advisable for customers with known
allergic reactions to nuts and nut derivatives and those who
may be potentially vulnerable to these allergies, such as
pregnant and nursing mothers, people with a weakened
immune system, the elderly, babies, and children, to avoid
dishes made with nuts and nut oils. It is also prudent to
check the labels of prepared ingredients for the possible
inclusion of nut derivatives.

# contents

# introduction

This book offers a new and flexible approach to meal-planning for busy cooks and lets you choose the recipe option that best fits the time you have available. Inside you will find 200 dishes that will inspire you and motivate you to get cooking every day of the year.

All the recipes take a maximum of 30 minutes to cook. Some take as little as 20 minutes and, amazingly, many take only 10 minutes.

On every page you'll find a main recipe plus a short-cut version or a fancier variation if you have a bit more time to spare. Whatever you go for, you'll find a huge range of super-quick recipes to get you through the week.

## one pot meals

With so many of us living busy lives these days, cooking dinner is enough of an effort without having to tackle a mountain of dishes afterwards. One pot dishes are simple to prepare—from an easy salad tossed together in a bowl, to quickly frying some meat and vegetables and then simmering in a flavorful liquid. All the recipes in this book require just one main cooking utensil, so once dinner is finished the clear-up is really easy.

## choosing the right dish

**Casserole dish**: A heavy casserole dish is perfect for many one pot dishes and there are plenty that are smart enough to bring from the stove to the table for a dinner party. They are best for making moist dishes like stews or curries. You can also find shallower casseroles that are great for cooking rice-based dishes. The best casseroles are made from cast iron, which is brilliant at retaining heat and ensuring even cooking. They can be pricy to buy, but they are an investment that should last you a lifetime.

**Saucepan**: Ideally, get a heavy pan so you can double up and use it for frying as well. A large pan will give you the space you need

to cook soup or pasta for the whole family, or any other recipe that requires a lot of liquid.

**Skillet**: To ensure that food doesn't burn when cooking, look out for pans with a heavy bottom. Sticking is often a problem when frying, so try using a cast-iron pan and heating it until it is smoking hot—the heat will help prevent sticking—or you can use a nonstick pan. Sauté pans are deeper than skillets, allowing you to fry more gently and making it easier to add a little stock or other liquid. You can also buy sauté pans with a lid, which allows you to steam food and keep it moist, or alternatively you can tightly cover the pan with foil. Skillets have shallower sides and are best used when you really want to brown something over an intensive heat, like a steak.

**Baking and roasting pans**: Some of the simplest one pan dishes are cooked in the oven, so after a little prep work your job is done. A ceramic baking dish worwwks well and many of these are elegant enough to bring to table. But a sturdy metal roasting pan is also useful. Try looking for versions with a handle, as this makes them easier to get out of the oven. To make sure your food gets browned in the oven, choose a pan that is shallow, otherwise the ingredients will simply steam.

**Ridged grill pan**: A grill pan will bring the great taste of an outdoor barbecue to your kitchen. The metal dish can be heated on the stovetop and the ridges will give your food that special seared look. Cooking like this can be smoky, so it's worth having an extractor fan

look for woks with a rounded bottom, but for electric or induction burners, go for a wok with a flat bottom so it won't tip over during cooking.

## using the best ingredients

**Meat**: Many one pot dishes use slower-cooking cuts taken from the shoulder or leg of the animal. These are tougher cuts and require a long and low simmering in the pot to produce tender meat. When time is of the essence you need to use quicker-cooking cuts such as loin. Taken from the middle of the animal, these cuts need to be cooked fast—if you leave them for a long time they toughen up and tend to dry out.

**Ready-cooked vegetables**: Ready-roasted vegetables are now widely available, and some grilled eggplant or zucchini will really lift a dish and save you lots of time and effort.

**Canned legumes:** Dried beans and legumes take time to cook from scratch, but are perfect for absorbing delicious flavors and filling you up. Luckily you can find most beans canned and they are simple to drain and rinse before using. You can find lentils in cans, but they are also available in microwavable pouches, which are quick to heat through.

**Ready-cooked rice and noodles**: You can now buy ready-cooked rice and noodles that are simple to make into a quick one

on. It's also a really healthy way to cook food. Don't add oil to the pan, rub a little oil over the surface of the food instead, then season and add to the pan.

**Wok**: You can cook large-portion meals in a wok, but make sure not to overcrowd the pan when stir-frying. Cut all the vegetables and meat to the same size so they cook quickly and evenly. Add items like noodles and rice at the end to get the maximum flavor. You can also use a wok for deep-fat frying, simmering, and steaming, if it has a lid. Heavy woks are a good investment as they will ensure food doesn't burn, but nonstick versions are also available. For a gas flame, pot supper. Cooked rice can be added or simply microwaved in the pack, while there is a large selection of noodles available to brighten up a stir-fry and couscous is the perfect quick-cooking ingredient.

**Prepared pastry**: Ready-made pastry is now widely available and you can also find ready-rolled pastry to make life easier still. Look out for pastry made with butter: it costs a little more, but the flavor is fantastic. In addition to puff and shortcrust pastry, try using phyllo pastry. These thin sheets, which crisp up in the oven, just need brushing over with melted butter or oil and can then be used to make savory or sweet dishes.

## the finishing touches

One pot dishes need to be packed full of flavor, so stock up on ingredients that will give your meals a sparkling finish such as herbs, spices, and cheese. Using just one pot makes life in the kitchen much simpler, but it's easy to add side dishes without creating more stress. Bread is great with most meals. Choose a baguette to mop up a soupy stew, or in the warmer months, whip up a salad to enjoy with your meal.

# poultry

# lentil & chicken stew

Serves **4**

Total cooking time **10 minutes**

1 tablespoon **olive oil**

2 **chicken breasts**, each
about 5 oz, thinly sliced

3 **celery sticks**, coarsely
chopped

4 **tomatoes**, coarsely
chopped

1¼ cups **ready-cooked Puy
lentils**

1 (14½ oz) can **diced
tomatoes**

1 **chicken bouillon cube**,
crumbled

⅔ cup **boiling water**

2 tablespoons chopped
**parsley**

**Heat** the oil in a medium-size, heavy skillet and cook
the chicken and celery for 5 minutes. Add the fresh
tomatoes and stir for 1 minute.

**Add** the lentils, canned tomatoes, and bouillon cube
together with the measured water. Bring to a boil and
keep at a boil for 2 minutes, stirring occasionally.

**Stir** in the chopped parsley and serve ladled into serving
bowls with crusty bread, if desired, to mop up the juices.

**For thick red lentil & chicken stew**, heat 1 tablespoon
olive oil and cook 2 × 5 oz thinly sliced chicken breasts,
1 large thinly sliced onion, and 4 coarsely chopped
celery sticks over moderately high heat for 5 minutes.
Add 4 coarsely chopped tomatoes, 1¼ cups red lentils,
1 (14½ oz) can diced tomatoes, and 2½ cups chicken
stock. Bring to a boil, reduce the heat, cover and
simmer, stirring occasionally, for 20 minutes or until
the lentils are soft and tender. Season with salt and
pepper to taste and stir in 6 tablespoons chopped
parsley. Serve with warm crusty bread. **Total cooking
time 30 minutes.**

# soy chicken with mushrooms

Serves **4**

Total cooking time **20 minutes**

4 small **skinless chicken breast fillets**

7 oz **mixed mushrooms**

5 tablespoons **soy sauce**

finely grated zest and juice of ½ **lime**

1 **chile**, sliced

1 **garlic clove**, chopped

1 teaspoon finely grated **fresh ginger root**

handful of chopped **fresh cilantro**, to garnish

boiled **jasmine rice**, to serve (optional)

**Set** a large steamer over a saucepan of gently simmering water. Place the chicken and mushrooms in a shallow, heatproof dish that will fit inside the steamer. Mix together the remaining ingredients and spoon over the chicken.

**Place** the dish in the steamer, cover, and cook for 15 minutes, until the chicken is just cooked through. Sprinkle with cilantro and serve with jasmine rice, if desired.

**For soy-fried noodles with chicken & oyster mushrooms**, heat a wok until smoking hot. Add 2 tablespoons vegetable oil and 10 oz thinly sliced chicken breast. Stir-fry for 5 minutes, then add 1 crushed garlic clove, 1 teaspoon finely grated fresh ginger root, and 7 oz oyster mushrooms. Cook for another 2 minutes. Stir in 10 oz ready-cooked egg noodles, 2 cups baby spinach leaves, and ¼ cup soy sauce mixed with 1 tablespoon sweet chili sauce. Heat through until piping hot and serve immediately. **Total cooking time 10 minutes.**

# chicken drumstick jambalaya

Serves **4**

Total cooking time **30 minutes**

1 tablespoon **sunflower oil**

8 **skinless chicken drumsticks**

1 **onion**, chopped

2 **garlic cloves**, crushed

2 **celery sticks**, sliced

1 **red chile**, seeded and chopped

1 **green bell pepper**, cored, seeded, and chopped

3 oz **chorizo sausage**, sliced

1 cup **American long-grain rice**

2 cups **chicken stock**

1 **bay leaf**

3 **tomatoes**, cut into wedges

dash of **Tabasco sauce**

**salt** and **pepper**

**Heat** the oil in a large sauté pan. Cut a few slashes across the thickest part of the drumsticks, add them to the pan and fry over high heat for 5 minutes, turning occasionally. Add the onion, garlic, celery, chile, and bell pepper and cook for another 2–3 minutes or until softened.

**Add** the chorizo, fry briefly, then add the rice, stirring to coat the grains in the pan juices. Pour in the bouillon, add the bay leaf, and bring to a boil. Cover, reduce the heat, and simmer for 20 minutes, stirring occasionally, until the stock has been absorbed and the rice is tender.

**Stir** in the tomatoes and Tabasco sauce and season to taste. Heat through for 3 minutes before serving.

**For quick chicken & chorizo stew**, pour 1 ½ cups ready-made tomato and roasted pepper pasta sauce into a saucepan. Add 7 oz chopped ready-cooked chicken, 3 oz sliced chorizo, and 1 (15 oz) can lima beans, rinsed and drained. Simmer for 5 minutes and serve with crusty bread. **Total cooking time 10 minutes.**

# thai red duck curry

Serves **4**

Total cooking time **30 minutes**

2 tablespoons **sunflower oil**

2 **garlic cloves**, crushed

1 teaspoon peeled and finely grated **fresh ginger root**

2 tablespoons **Thai red curry paste**

13 oz **skinless duck breasts**, thinly sliced

2⅔ cups **coconut milk**

7 oz **snow peas**, halved lengthwise

¾ cup hot **chicken stock**

4 **kaffir lime leaves**

2 teaspoons grated **palm sugar** or **sugar**

2 **lemon grass stalks**, bruised

**salt** and **pepper**

handful of chopped **fresh cilantro**, to garnish

steamed **jasmine rice**, to serve

**Heat** the oil in a large wok or skillet until hot, add the garlic and ginger and stir-fry over high heat for 20–30 seconds. Stir in the curry paste and stir-fry for 30 seconds, then add the duck and stir-fry for another 4–5 minutes.

**Stir** in the coconut milk, snow peas, stock, lime leaves, sugar, and lemon grass and bring to a boil, then reduce the heat to medium and cook, uncovered, for 15–20 minutes, stirring occasionally, until the duck is cooked through. Season to taste.

**Ladle** into bowls, sprinkle with chopped cilantro, and serve with steamed jasmine rice.

**For Thai-style red duck salad**, thinly slice 4 smoked duck breasts and put in a large salad bowl with a large handful of mixed salad leaves. Mix together 1 teaspoon Thai red curry paste, 6 tablespoons light olive oil, 2 teaspoons honey, and 3 tablespoons red wine vinegar in a bowl, then season. Pour the dressing over the salad, toss to mix well and serve with warm crusty bread. **Total cooking time 10 minutes.**

# french-style chicken stew

Serves **4**

Total cooking time **20 minutes**

1 **leek**, sliced

4 **boneless, skinless chicken thighs**, cut into chunks

13 oz small **new potatoes**, halved

1 **carrot**, sliced

1²⁄₃ cups hot **chicken stock**

3 tablespoons **dry white wine**

²⁄₃ cup **frozen peas**, defrosted

2 tablespoons **sour cream**

**salt** and **pepper**

handful of chopped **tarragon**, to garnish

**Place** the leek, chicken, potatoes, and carrot in a large saucepan. Pour in the bouillon and wine and season with salt and pepper to taste.

**Bring** to a boil, then reduce the heat and simmer for 15 minutes, until just cooked through.

**Stir** in the peas and sour cream and heat through. Sprinkle with the tarragon and serve immediately.

**For chicken sauté with peas, lettuce & tarragon**, heat 1 tablespoon oil in a saucepan. Add 10 oz thinly sliced chicken and cook for 2 minutes until golden. Add 1 crushed garlic clove and cook for another 30 seconds. Pour in 2 tablespoons dry white wine and bubble for 1 minute, then add 3 tablespoons chicken stock and boil hard for 2 minutes. Stir in ²⁄₃ cup defrosted frozen peas, 1 sliced baby romaine lettuce, and 2 tablespoons sour cream, season to taste and heat through. Sprinkle with chopped tarragon and serve with lightly toasted baguette slices. **Total cooking time 10 minutes.**

# chicken & corn chowder

Serves **4**
Total cooking time **10 minutes**

1 (14¾ oz) can **cream-style corn**
1¾ cups **milk**
6 oz **ready-cooked chicken**, torn into pieces
¾ cup **frozen corn kernels**
2 **scallions**, chopped
2 teaspoons **cornstarch**
**salt** and **pepper**
**crusty bread**, to serve

**Place** the cream-style corn in a saucepan with the milk and heat, stirring.

**Add** the chicken, corn kernels, and scallions and season to taste. Simmer for 5 minutes, stirring occasionally.

**Blend** the cornstarch with 1 tablespoon water, pour into the soup and stir to thicken. Ladle into bowls and serve with crusty bread.

**For chicken, bacon & corn chowder**, fry 2 chopped slices of bacon with 1 chopped onion and 2 chopped medium potatoes in a pat of butter for 5 minutes. Pour in 2 cups milk and simmer for 10 minutes. Stir in ¾ cup frozen corn kernels and 6 oz chopped ready-cooked chicken. Season to taste, heat through and serve sprinkled with chopped fresh parsley. **Total cooking time 20 minutes.**

# turkey with pancetta & beans

Serves **4**

Total cooking time **30 minutes**

handful of chopped **rosemary**
handful of chopped **parsley**
2 tablespoons **butter**,
  softened
1¾ lb **turkey breast joint**
6 **garlic cloves**
3 tablespoons **dry white wine**
3 tablespoons hot **chicken
  stock**
4 **pancetta slices**
2 (15 oz) cans **lima beans**,
  rinsed and drained
handful of **sundried tomatoes**,
  coarsely chopped
3 tablespoons **heavy cream**
**salt** and **pepper**

**Mix** together the rosemary, three-quarters of the parsley, and the butter and smear over the turkey joint. Season with salt and pepper to taste.

**Place** in a roasting pan with the garlic cloves, pour the wine and stock into the pan, and arrange the pancetta on top of the turkey. Place in a preheated oven, 425°F, for 25 minutes.

**Put** the beans, tomatoes, and cream into the roasting pan, topping up with a little water if necessary. Season to taste, then return to the oven for another 3–5 minutes or until the turkey is cooked through and the beans are warm.

**Cut** the turkey into slices and arrange on plates with the crispy pancetta and the beans, sprinkled with the remaining parsley.

**For turkey, bacon & bean stew**, mix 13 oz ground turkey with 2 finely chopped scallions, 1 finely chopped bacon slice, and 1 egg yolk and season well. Roll the mixture into small balls. Heat 1 tablespoon oil in a deep skillet. Fry the balls for 5 minutes until golden all over. Stir in 1 crushed garlic clove, then add ½ cup canned diced tomatoes and simmer for 5–10 minutes, until the turkey balls are cooked through. Stir in 1 (14 oz) can lima beans, rinsed and drained, and heat through. Season to taste and sprinkle with parsley to serve. **Total cooking time 20 minutes.**

# chicken & spinach stew

Serves **4**

Total cooking time **20 minutes**

1¼ lb **skinless, boneless chicken thighs,** thinly sliced

2 teaspoons **ground cumin**

1 teaspoon **ground ginger**

2 tablespoons **olive oil**

1 tablespoon **tomato paste**

2 (14½ oz) cans **cherry tomatoes**

¼ cup **raisins**

1¼ cups **ready-cooked Puy lentils**

1 teaspoon grated **lemon** zest

3 cups **baby spinach**

**salt** and **pepper**

handful of chopped **parsley,** to garnish

steamed **couscous** or **rice,** to serve

**Mix** the chicken with the ground spices until well coated. Heat the olive oil in a large saucepan or flameproof casserole dish, then add the chicken and cook for 2–3 minutes, until lightly browned.

**Stir** in the tomato paste, tomatoes, raisins, lentils, and lemon zest, season with salt and pepper and simmer gently for about 12 minutes, until thickened slightly and the chicken is cooked.

**Add** the spinach and stir until wilted. Ladle the stew into bowls, then sprinkle with parsley and serve with steamed couscous or rice.

**For chicken & rice soup with lemon**, heat 2 tablespoons oil in a large saucepan and cook 4 sliced scallions and 2 chopped garlic cloves over medium heat for 2–3 minutes, to soften. Add 7 oz thinly sliced, skinless chicken breast and cook for 3–4 minutes, until lightly browned all over. Add ¾ cup washed long-grain rice and stir to coat in the oil. Pour 5 cups of good-quality, hot chicken or vegetable stock into the pan, season to taste, add a pinch of freshly grated nutmeg, then simmer for about 15 minutes, until the rice is tender. Stir 3 cups mixed watercress and spinach leaves, chopped, into the soup and stir for 1–2 minutes, until the leaves have wilted. Ladle into bowls and serve with lemon wedges. **Total cooking time 30 minutes.**

# spiced roast chicken with lime

Serves **4**

Total cooking time **30 minutes**

8 small **skinless chicken thighs**

1 tablespoon **harissa**

¼ cup **honey**

2 **limes**, cut into wedges

1 **red bell pepper**, cored, seeded, and cut into large chunks

2 **zucchini**, cut into chunks

1 **onion**, cut into wedges

10 oz **new potatoes**, halved if large

1 tablespoon **olive oil**

**salt** and **pepper**

**Cut** a few slashes across each chicken thigh. Mix together the harissa and honey and rub all over the chicken thighs. Place in a roasting pan large enough to spread everything out in a single layer, with the lime wedges, bell pepper, zucchini, onion, and potatoes.

**Drizzle** over the oil, season, and roast in a preheated oven, 425°F, for 25 minutes, turning occasionally, or until the chicken is cooked and the vegetables are tender. Serve with the juice of the lime wedges squeezed over the chicken.

**For pan-fried spicy chicken**, cut 8 small skinless chicken thigh fillets into strips and coat in a mixture of 1 tablespoon harissa and 1 tablespoon honey. Heat 1 tablespoon sunflower oil in a large skillet, add the chicken and fry over medium heat for 5 minutes. Add 1 cored, seeded, and chopped red bell pepper, 2 chopped zucchini, 1 onion, cut into thin wedges, and 2 limes, cut into wedges. Cook for 10 minutes, stirring occasionally, or until the chicken is cooked and the vegetables are tender. Serve with new potatoes. **Total cooking time 20 minutes.**

# mango & coconut curry

Serves **4**

Total cooking time **20 minutes**

1 tablespoon **vegetable oil**

1 large **onion**, chopped

1 lb cubed **chicken meat**

1 large, ripe **mango**, peeled, pitted, and cut into chunks

1 teaspoon **ground coriander**

1 teaspoon **ground cumin**

2 tablespoons **korma curry paste**

1⅔ cups **coconut milk**

1¼ cups **chicken stock**

6 tablespoons chopped **fresh cilantro**

1 tablespoon **cornstarch**

**To serve** (optional)

**steamed rice**

**pappadams**

**Heat** the oil in a large, heavy skillet or wok and cook the onion and chicken over high heat for 5 minutes or until golden and beginning to soften.

**Add** the chopped mango, spices, and curry paste and stir for a few seconds before adding the coconut milk and stock. Bring to a boil, then reduce the heat and simmer, uncovered and stirring occasionally, for 10–12 minutes, then add the fresh cilantro.

**Blend** the cornstarch with 2 tablespoons water, pour into the hot curry and stir well to thicken. Serve with rice and pappadams, if desired.

**For pulpy mango & chicken curry**, heat 1 tablespoon oil in a large, heavy skillet and cook 12 oz cubed chicken for 2 minutes. Add 2 tablespoons curry paste, 1¼ cups canned mango pulp, and 1⅔ cups coconut milk. Bring to a boil, reduce the heat and simmer for 7 minutes. Add 1½ cups frozen peas for the final 3 minutes of cooking. Serve with toasted naan bread fingers. **Total cooking time 10 minutes.**

# chicken & chorizo with lentils

Serves **2**

Total cooking time **10 minutes**

1 tablespoon **olive oil**

1 small **onion**, thinly sliced

4 oz **chorizo sausage**, thinly sliced

10 oz **skinless chicken breast fillets**, cubed

1¼ cups **ready-cooked green lentils**

2 tablespoons **thyme leaves**

⅔ cup hot **chicken stock**

1 tablespoon **Dijon mustard**

**salt** and **pepper**

**crusty bread**, to serve (optional)

**Heat** the oil in a large skillet, add the onion, chorizo, and chicken and cook over medium-high heat for 5–7 minutes, stirring occasionally, until golden and the chicken is cooked through.

**Add** the lentils, thyme, stock, and mustard and stir well to combine, then cook for another 2 minutes until boiling. Season well with pepper and a little salt to taste. Serve with crusty bread, if desired.

**For chicken, chorizo & lentil soup**, heat 1 tablespoon olive oil in a large saucepan, add 1 coarsely chopped onion, 4 oz diced chorizo sausage, and 5 oz coarsely cubed skinless chicken breast fillets and cook for 4–5 minutes, until golden and the chicken is cooked through. Add ¾ cup green lentils and 2 cups hot chicken stock and bring to a boil. Reduce the heat, cover, and simmer for 20 minutes, until the lentils are tender. Stir in 1 tablespoon Dijon mustard and season well. Transfer the mixture to a food processor and blend until almost smooth. Serve with crusty bread. **Total cooking time 30 minutes.**

# chicken & tomato polenta pie

Serves **4**

Total cooking time **30 minutes**

2 tablespoons **olive oil**

10 oz **skinless chicken
breast fillets**, cubed

2 **garlic cloves**, finely chopped

1 teaspoon **tomato paste**

1 (14½ oz) can **diced
tomatoes**

pinch of **dried red pepper
flakes**

handful of chopped **basil**

1 **zucchini**, sliced

1 lb **ready-cooked polenta**,
cut into ½ inch slices

¼ cup grated **Parmesan
cheese**

**salt** and **pepper**

**Heat** the oil in a shallow, flameproof casserole dish.
Add the chicken, season with salt and pepper to taste,
and cook for 3–4 minutes, until starting to turn golden,
then remove from the dish and set aside.

**Add** the garlic to the dish, cook for 1 minute, then
add the tomato paste and tomatoes. Stir in the pepper
flakes and basil, bring to a boil, then reduce the heat
and simmer for 10 minutes.

**Return** the chicken to the dish along with the zucchini
and cook for another 5–10 minutes, until the chicken
is just cooked through.

**Arrange** the polenta slices on top of the chicken
mixture, then sprinkle with the Parmesan. Cook under
a preheated hot broiler for 5 minutes or until golden
and bubbling.

**For corn, tomato & chicken salad**, heat 1 tablespoon
olive oil in a skillet. Add ½ cup fresh or canned corn
kernels and cook for 3 minutes, until browned. Chop
1 romaine lettuce and toss with 2 chopped tomatoes
and 2 ready-cooked chicken breasts, torn into shreds.
Mix 3 tablespoons buttermilk with 1 teaspoon cider
vinegar and 1 teaspoon sugar and season to taste.
Sprinkle the corn kernels over the salad, then drizzle
over the buttermilk dressing and serve immediately.
**Total cooking time 10 minutes.**

# duck & figs with watercress salad

Serves **4**

Total cooking time **20 minutes**

4 **duck breast fillets**
4 **figs**, halved
½ teaspoon **ground cinnamon**
1 tablespoon **balsamic vinegar**
1 teaspoon **honey**
finely grated zest and juice of ½ **orange**
2½ cups **watercress**
1 **endive head**, leaves separated
**salt** and **pepper**

**Use** a sharp knife to score a criss-cross pattern on the skin of the duck and season with salt and pepper to taste. Heat a large skillet until hot, add the duck, skin side down, and cook for 7 minutes. Pour away the excess oil and turn the duck over. Arrange the figs in the pan and cook for another 5–7 minutes, until the duck is cooked through and the figs softened.

**Remove** the duck from the pan and cut into thick slices. Tip away any excess fat, then add the cinnamon, vinegar, honey, and orange zest and juice to the pan and swirl around.

**Divide** the watercress and endive among plates, place the figs and sliced duck on top, then spoon over the warm dressing and serve immediately.

**For smoked duck, orange & fig salad**, cut 4 figs in half, drizzle with a little olive oil and 1 teaspoon balsamic vinegar, then cook under a preheated hot broiler for 2 minutes on each side until lightly charred. Toss 3½ cups watercress with 1 tablespoon sherry vinegar and 3 tablespoons olive oil and divide between serving plates. Peel 1 orange and cut into segments, then arrange on the plates with the broiled figs and 3½ oz ready-made sliced smoked duck breast. **Total cooking time 10 minutes.**

# greek chicken stifado

Serves **2**

Total cooking time **30 minutes**

3 tablespoons **olive oil**

2 **chicken quarters**

2 **shallots**, peeled and cut
in half

1 **fennel bulb**, trimmed and
cut into slim wedges

1 (14 oz) can **artichokes**,
drained and halved

⅓ cup **kalamata olives**, pitted

3 tablespoons **tomato paste**

2 **tomatoes**, coarsely chopped

1 tablespoon **rosemary
leaves**

1¼ cups hot **chicken stock**

warm **crusty bread**, to serve
(optional)

**Heat** the oil in a large skillet, add the chicken, skin side down, shallots, and fennel wedges and cook over medium-high heat for 10 minutes until the chicken is golden.

**Turn** the chicken over and add the artichokes, olives, tomato paste, tomatoes, rosemary, and stock and stir well, then cover tightly and simmer for 15–20 minutes, until the chicken is cooked through and the tomatoes have softened, adding a little water if the sauce is too thick. Serve with warm crusty bread to mop up the juices, if desired.

### For chicken, artichoke & olive pan-fry, heat
2 tablespoons olive oil in a large skillet, add 10 oz thinly sliced skinless chicken breast fillets and cook over high heat until golden, then add 1 teaspoon rosemary leaves, 1 (14 oz) can artichokes, drained and halved, ½ cup pitted black ripe olives, and 1¼ cups ready-made tomato pasta sauce with vegetables and cook for 5 minutes, until piping hot and the chicken is cooked through. Serve with ready-cooked rice or warm crusty bread to mop up the juices. **Total cooking time 10 minutes.**

# jerk chicken & sweet potato soup

Serves **4–6**

Total cooking time **20 minutes**

2 tablespoons **vegetable oil**

1 **red onion**, chopped

1 **celery stick**, chopped

1 inch piece of **fresh ginger root**, peeled and chopped

1 tablespoon **jerk seasoning**

2 lb **sweet potato**, chopped (or use a mixture of sweet potato and butternut squash)

5 cups hot **chicken stock**

2 tablespoons **lime juice**

8 oz **ready-cooked chicken**, shredded

**salt** and **pepper**

thinly sliced **scallions**, to garnish

**Heat** the vegetable oil in a large saucepan and fry the onion, celery, and ginger for 4–5 minutes, until beginning to soften. Add the jerk seasoning, then mix in the sweet potato and stir over the heat for 1 minute.

**Pour** the chicken stock into the pan and simmer over medium heat for about 12 minutes, until the potato is tender. Blend to the desired consistency, then stir in the lime juice and season with salt and pepper to taste.

**Ladle** the soup into bowls and top each with a handful of the shredded chicken. Garnish with scallions and serve.

**For quick jerk chicken broth**, heat 2 tablespoons vegetable oil in a large saucepan over medium heat and add 3 sliced scallions and 1 tablespoon peeled and grated fresh ginger root. Cook for 1–2 minutes, until softened. Stir in 1 tablespoon jerk seasoning and cook for 1 minute before pouring in 5 cups hot chicken stock. Simmer for 3–4 minutes, then take off the heat and stir in 8 oz shredded ready-cooked chicken and 1–2 tablespoons lime juice. Ladle into bowls and serve, garnished with extra sliced scallions, if desired. **Total cooking time 10 minutes.**

# chicken with lemon & olives

Serves **4**

Total cooking time **30 minutes**

pinch of **saffron threads**

4 **chicken drumsticks** and
   4 small **chicken thighs**,
   skinned

1 **lemon**, halved

2 tablespoons **honey**

⅔ cup **dry white wine**

⅔ cup **green olives**

**salt** and **pepper**

2 tablespoons coarsely
   chopped **flat-leaf parsley**,
   to garnish

**To serve** (optional)
**new potatoes**
**green beans**

**Soak** the saffron in 1 tablespoon boiling water. Cut a couple of slashes across the top of each piece of chicken and season with salt and pepper. Spread out the chicken in a large roasting pan or ovenproof dish and squeeze over the lemon halves.

**Drizzle** over the honey, pour over the saffron threads and soaking water, and add the white wine. Roast in a preheated oven, 425°F, for 20 minutes, basting with the juices occasionally. Add the olives and cook for another 5 minutes, until the chicken is cooked.

**Sprinkle** with parsley and serve with new potatoes and green beans, if desired.

**For lemon chicken stir-fry**, heat 1 tablespoon sunflower oil in a wok or large skillet, add 13½ oz chicken tenders and stir-fry over high heat for 5 minutes. Add 1 tablespoon honey, ¼ cup lemon juice, ¼ cup dry white wine, and ⅔ cup green olives. Heat through for 2 minutes, season, and serve with ready-made couscous salad. **Total cooking time 10 minutes.**

# cken & boston beans

Serves **4**

Total cooking time **10 minutes**

1 tablespoon **olive oil**

2 **chicken breasts**, each about
   5 oz, thinly sliced

1 **onion**, thinly sliced

1 tablespoon **dark molasses**

1 tablespoon **whole-grain
   mustard**

1 tablespoon **packed dark
   brown sugar**

1 (14½ oz) can **diced
   tomatoes**

1 (16 oz) can **baked beans**

3 tablespoons chopped
   **parsley**

**pepper**

4 thick slices **whole-wheat
   toast**, to serve

**Heat** the oil in a medium, heavy saucepan and cook the chicken and onion over moderate heat for 3–4 minutes.

**Add** the molasses, mustard, sugar, and tomatoes, bring to a boil and simmer for 2 minutes before adding the beans, then stir in the parsley and heat through for 1 minute.

**Spoon** the mixture onto the slices of whole-wheat toast, season with pepper, and serve immediately.

**For paprika Boston baked beans with chicken & bacon**, heat 2 tablespoons olive oil in a large skillet and cook 1 thinly sliced onion, 2 thinly sliced chicken breasts, and 4 slices of chopped bacon for 5 minutes or until golden, soft, and cooked through. Add 1 teaspoon paprika, 1 tablespoon molasses, 1 tablespoon whole-grain mustard, and 2 tablespoons packed dark brown sugar and stir well. Stir in 1 (14½ oz) can diced tomatoes and 2 (15 oz) cans cannellini beans, rinsed and drained. Bring to a boil, cover, and simmer for 10 minutes, removing the lid for the final 2 minutes. Stir through 2 tablespoons chopped parsley and serve. **Total cooking time 20 minutes.**

# chicken with cashews

Serves **2**

Total cooking time **10 minutes**

⅓ cup **unsalted cashew nuts**

1 teaspoon **sesame oil**

2 **skinless chicken breast fillets**, cut into strips

1 **garlic clove**, crushed

½ inch piece **fresh ginger root**, grated

4 oz **oyster mushrooms**, sliced

4 **scallions**, thickly sliced diagonally

1 cup **frozen soy beans**

6 tablespoons **oyster sauce**

**Heat** a wok or large skillet until hot, add the cashew nuts and cook, stirring, for 1 minute or until golden, taking care not to let them burn. Remove them from the pan to a plate and set aside.

**Place** the oil in the pan along with the chicken strips and cook, stirring, for 3 minutes or until browned and cooked through.

**Add** the garlic, ginger, mushrooms, and scallions and cook for 2 minutes or until the mushrooms and scallions are just tender. Add the soy beans and oyster sauce, bring to a boil and simmer for 2 minutes, adding a little water if the mixture is too dry. Sprinkle over the toasted cashew nuts before serving.

**For ginger chicken & rice stir-fry**, cook 2 chopped skinless chicken breast fillets in a large skillet with 1 teaspoon sunflower oil, 1 teaspoon garlic paste, 1 teaspoon ginger paste, 4 sliced scallions, and 1 cup frozen soy beans. Add 2 cups ready-cooked egg-fried rice and a dash of sweet chili sauce and soy sauce. Stir-fry until hot. **Total cooking time 10 minutes.**

# paprika chicken with peppers

Serves **4**

Total cooking time **10 minutes**

1 tablespoon **sunflower oil**
13 oz **chicken tenders**
1 teaspoon **garlic paste**
1 tablespoon **paprika**
1 ⅓ cups **frozen sliced mixed sweet peppers**
1 tablespoon **tomato paste**
⅔ cup **sour cream**
**salt** and **pepper**
**tagliatelle**, to serve

**Heat** the oil in a large skillet, add the chicken, and stir-fry over high heat for 5 minutes. Add the garlic paste, paprika, peppers, and tomato paste and cook, stirring, for 3 minutes.

**Stir** in the sour cream, season with salt and pepper to taste and heat through. Serve with tagliatelle.

**For paprika chicken casserole,** fry 4 skinless chicken breast fillets in 1 tablespoon sunflower oil for 5 minutes, turning once, until golden. Add 1 chopped onion and 1 cored, seeded, and chopped green bell pepper, fry for 3 minutes then stir in 1 tablespoon paprika, 1 tablespoon tomato paste, and 1 (14½ oz) can diced tomatoes. Simmer for 15 minutes, season to taste and stir in ⅔ cup sour cream. Serve with mashed potato. **Total cooking time 30 minutes.**

# turkey tikka skewers

Serves **4**

Total cooking time **20 minutes**

3 tablespoons **tikka masala curry paste**

2 tablespoons **plain yogurt**

1 lb **cubed turkey breast**

1 large **onion**, cut into bite-size pieces

1 large **green bell pepper**, cored, seeded, and cut into bite-size pieces

**To serve** (optional)
**basmati** or **long-grain rice**
**mango chutney**

**In** a bowl, mix the curry paste with the yogurt, then add the cubed turkey. Mix well to coat, then thread onto 4–8 metal or presoaked wooden skewers with the chunks of onion and pepper. Arrange on the rack of a foil-lined broiler tray.

**Cook** under a preheated medium broiler for 12–15 minutes, turning occasionally, until thoroughly cooked and lightly charred.

**Serve** hot with basmati or long-grain rice and mango chutney, if desired.

**For turkey tikka masala**, heat 2 tablespoons vegetable oil in a large saucepan and cook 1 large coarsely chopped onion and 1 cored, seeded, and diced green or red bell pepper for 7–8 minutes, until softened. Stir ¼ cup tikka masala curry paste into the pan followed by 13 oz cubed turkey breast. Stir to combine and seal the turkey, then add 1 (14½ oz) can diced tomatoes and 1¼ cups water. Bring to a boil, then reduce the heat and simmer gently, uncovered, for 12–15 minutes, until the turkey is thoroughly cooked and the sauce has thickened. Stir ½ cup full-fat plain yogurt into the curry before serving with basmati or long-grain rice. **Total cooking time 30 minutes.**

# chicken with warm lentils & kale

Serves **4**

Total cooking time **20 minutes**

2 tablespoons **olive oil**

4 **skinless chicken breast fillets**

1 **garlic clove**, sliced

1¼ cups chopped **kale**

1¼ cups ready-cooked **Puy lentils**

2 tablespoons **lemon juice**

3 oz **sundried tomatoes in oil**, drained

3 oz **soft goat cheese**, crumbled

**salt** and **pepper**

**Heat** half the oil in a large skillet. Add the chicken, season with salt and pepper to taste and cook for 5 minutes, then turn over and cook for 2 minutes, until golden all over.

**Add** the remaining oil to the pan along with the garlic, kale, and a splash of water. Cover and cook for 7 minutes, until the kale is tender and the chicken cooked through.

**Stir** in the lentils and heat through, then add the lemon juice and tomatoes. Check and adjust the seasoning if necessary.

**Cut** the chicken into thick slices and arrange on plates with the lentils. Sprinkle with the goat cheese and serve immediately.

**For hearty lentil, kale & chicken soup**, heat 2 tablespoons olive oil in a saucepan. Add 1 finely chopped onion and cook gently for 5 minutes, then add 2 chopped garlic cloves, 1 teaspoon tomato paste, and a pinch of dried red pepper flakes and cook for 1 minute more. Pour in 7 cups chicken stock and bring to a boil. Add ¾ cup dried red lentils and simmer for 5 minutes. Skim off any scum that rises to the surface, add 7 oz cubed chicken breast, and cook for another 5 minutes. Add 1¼ cups chopped kale and simmer for 7 minutes, until tender. Season to taste and serve in bowls with crusty bread. **Total cooking time 30 minutes.**

# chicken, mushroom & dill pie

Serves **4**

Total cooking time **30 minutes**

1 tablespoon **vegetable oil**

1 **onion**, finely chopped

10 oz **skinless chicken breast fillets**, cubed

5 oz **mushrooms**, halved if large

3 tablespoons **dry white wine**

5 tablespoons **sour cream**

finely grated zest of 1 **lemon**

handful of chopped **dill weed**

3 large **phyllo pastry sheets**

3 tablespoons **butter**, melted

**salt** and **pepper**

**Heat** the oil in a shallow, ovenproof casserole dish. Add the onion and cook for 2 minutes, then stir in the chicken and cook for another 5 minutes. Add the mushrooms and continue to cook for 1 minute, until starting to soften.

**Pour** in the wine, cook until it has bubbled away, then stir in the sour cream, lemon zest, and dill and remove from the heat. Season with salt and pepper to taste.

**Meanwhile,** unwrap the phyllo pastry and cover with a piece of damp paper towel until ready to use it. Working quickly, brush 1 sheet with melted butter and cut into 3 long strips. Arrange the strips on top of the chicken, scrunching it up a little. Repeat with the remaining pastry until the chicken is covered.

**Brush** all over with any remaining butter, then place in a preheated oven, 400°F, for 15–20 minutes until the phyllo pastry is crisp and the chicken is cooked through.

**For chicken & wild mushrooms in a creamy dill sauce**, heat 1 tablespoon olive oil in a skillet. Add 1 sliced onion and cook for 5 minutes, until softened. Stir in 1 crushed garlic clove and 5 oz mixed wild mushrooms. Cook for 3 minutes, then add 2 ready-cooked chicken breasts, torn into shreds, 3 tablespoons sour cream, and 2 tablespoons chicken stock. Heat through, then add a handful of chopped dill weed and a good squeeze of lemon juice. Serve with garlic bread. **Total cooking time 10 minutes.**

# chicken with mascarpone

Serves **4**

Total cooking time **20 minutes**

¼ cup **mascarpone cheese**

4 teaspoons **ready-made fresh green pesto**

4 **skinless chicken breast fillets**

3 tablespoons **olive oil**

1 cup **dried bread crumbs**

5 oz **cherry tomatoes**

3 tablespoons **toasted pine nuts**

**salt** and **pepper**

**crusty bread**, to serve (optional)

**Mix** together the mascarpone and pesto. Use a small, sharp knife to make a horizontal slit in the side of each chicken breast to form a pocket. Fill the pockets with the mascarpone mixture.

**Season** the chicken and rub with 1 tablespoon of the oil, then turn in the bread crumbs until well coated. Place on a baking sheet, drizzle over another tablespoon of oil, and cook in a preheated oven, 400°F, for 10 minutes.

**Add** the tomatoes to the baking sheet, season and drizzle with the remaining oil. Return to the oven for another 5 minutes or until the chicken is cooked through. Sprinkle with the pine nuts and serve with crusty bread, if desired.

### For chicken pizza melts with cheese & tomatoes,

cut 2 skinless chicken breast fillets in half horizontally and place on a lightly greased baking sheet. Top each with a slice of tomato and a slice of mozzarella cheese, then season with salt and pepper to taste. Cook under a preheated hot broiler for 7 minutes or until the cheese has melted and the chicken is cooked through. Serve in burger buns with a few salad leaves. **Total cooking time 10 minutes.**

# chicken ratatouille

Serves **4**

Total cooking time **30 minutes**

8 small **skinless chicken thighs**
1 tablespoon **olive oil**
1 **onion**, chopped
1 **eggplant**, cut into bite-size chunks
1 **green bell pepper**, cored, seeded, and cut into bite-sized chunks
1 **red bell pepper**, cored, seeded, and cut into bite-size chunks
2 **zucchini**, chopped
1 **garlic clove**, crushed
1 (14½ oz) can **diced tomatoes**
pinch of **sugar**
handful of **basil**, coarsely torn
**salt** and **pepper**

**Cut** a couple of slashes across each chicken thigh and season with salt and pepper. Heat the oil in a large deep skillet, add the chicken and cook over high heat for 5 minutes, turning occasionally.

**Add** the onion, eggplant, peppers, zucchini, and garlic and cook for 10 minutes or until softened, adding a little water if the mixture becomes too dry.

**Pour** in the tomatoes, add the sugar, season to taste, and bring to a boil, stirring. Reduce the heat, cover and simmer for 15 minutes, stirring occasionally. Stir in the basil and serve.

**For chicken ratatouille with lentils**, chop 4 boneless, skinless chicken breasts and fry in 1 tablespoon olive oil for 5 minutes. Add 1 chopped eggplant, 2 chopped zucchini, 2 drained and chopped roasted red peppers from a jar, 1 (14½ oz) can diced tomatoes with garlic and herbs, and 1 (14½ oz) can green lentils, rinsed and drained. Bring to a boil, reduce the heat, cover and simmer for 10 minutes. Sprinkle with chopped basil before serving. **Total cooking time 20 minutes.**

meat

# baked sausages with apples

Serves **4**

Total cooking time **30 minutes**

3 **red onions**, cut into wedges

3 **red apples**, cored and cut
into 6 wedges

7 oz **baby carrots**, scrubbed

3 **potatoes**, peeled and cut
into small cubes

¼ cup **olive oil**

12 good-quality **pork
sausages**

2 tablespoons chopped **sage
leaves**

1 tablespoon **rosemary
leaves**

3 tablespoons **honey**

**salt** and **pepper**

**Arrange** the wedges of onion and apple in a large,
shallow roasting pan with the carrots and potatoes.
Drizzle over the oil, then toss well to lightly coat all
the vegetables in the oil. Season generously with salt
and pepper. Arrange the sausages in and around the
vegetables, sprinkle with the herbs and toss again.

**Place** in a preheated oven, 400°F, for 20–22 minutes,
until golden and cooked through.

**Remove** from the oven and drizzle over the honey.
Toss all the vegetables and sausages in the honey
and serve.

**For quick pork, apple & onion stir-fry**, cut 8 oz pork
tenderloin into very thin slices. Heat 2 tablespoons
olive oil in a large wok or heavy skillet and stir-fry the
pork over high heat for 2–3 minutes. Add 2 cored
apples and 2 red onions, each cut into slim wedges,
and stir-fry for 3–4 minutes, until browned and softened.
Add 1 tablespoon chopped sage leaves or rosemary
and toss to mix. Serve in warm ciabatta with plenty of
Dijon mustard. **Total cooking time 10 minutes.**

# italian beans with pancetta

Serves **4**

Total cooking time **10 minutes**

3 tablespoons **extra virgin
  olive oil**, plus extra to drizzle
10 oz **cubed pancetta**
3 **banana shallots**, chopped
2 teaspoons chopped **thyme**
2 (14 oz) cans **cranberry
  beans**, rinsed and drained
1 (15 oz) can **cannellini
  beans**, rinsed and drained
¾ cup **vegetable stock**
**salt** and **pepper**

**To serve**
**crusty bread**
**Parmesan cheese**, grated
chopped **parsley**

**Heat** the oil in a heavy skillet and fry the pancetta over high heat for 2–3 minutes, until golden. Reduce the heat slightly, add the shallots and thyme and cook for another 2–3 minutes, stirring occasionally, until just softened.

**Add** the beans and vegetable stock, season with a pinch of salt and plenty of pepper and simmer over medium heat for 2–3 minutes, until tender.

**Spoon** into bowls, drizzle over a little extra olive oil, and serve immediately with crusty bread, plenty of Parmesan, and chopped parsley.

**For chunky Italian stew with pancetta**, heat 2 tablespoons olive oil in a large saucepan or flameproof casserole dish over medium-high heat and add 7 oz cubed pancetta, 1 chopped onion, 2 chopped garlic cloves, 2 sliced celery sticks, and 2 diced carrots. Cook for 5–6 minutes, until beginning to color. Add 2 diced potatoes, 1 (14½ oz) can plum tomatoes, coarsely chopped, 1 (15 oz) can cannellini or cranberry beans, rinsed and drained, 1 teaspoon dried oregano, and 3 cups hot vegetable or chicken stock. Season generously and simmer over medium heat for about 15 minutes before adding 2 oz macaroni or other small pasta. Cook for another 5–6 minutes, until the pasta and vegetables are tender. Ladle into shallow bowls and serve as above. **Total cooking time 30 minutes.**

# pork, red pepper & pea curry

Serves **4**

Total cooking time **30 minutes**

3 tablespoons **vegetable oil**

2 teaspoons **cumin seeds**

2 **onions**, finely chopped

1 tablespoon peeled and
   grated **fresh ginger root**

1 tablespoon grated **garlic**

1 lb **ground pork**

2 tablespoons **ground
   coriander**

1 tablespoon **ground cumin**

1 tablespoon **garam masala**

1 **red bell pepper**, cored,
   seeded, and finely chopped

⅔ cup **frozen peas**

2 **ripe tomatoes**, finely
   chopped

juice of ½ **lime**

**salt**

handful of chopped **fresh
   cilantro**, to garnish

**To serve**

**plain yogurt**

**warm parathas** or **chapattis**
   (optional)

**Heat** the oil in a large wok or skillet until hot, add the cumin seeds and stir-fry over medium heat for 1 minute, then add the onions and stir-fry for another 3–4 minutes, until softened. Add the ginger and garlic and continue to stir-fry for 1 minute.

**Add** the pork and all the ground spices, season with salt and stir-fry for 8–10 minutes or until the pork is browned and cooked through. Stir in the bell pepper, peas, and tomatoes and stir-fry for another 3–4 minutes or until the vegetables are tender. Remove from the heat and stir in the lime juice.

**Sprinkle** with chopped cilantro and serve with a dollop of yogurt and warm parathas or chapattis, if desired.

**For Vietnamese-style pork baguettes**, prepare the cooked pork mixture as above. Meanwhile, split 2 warmed baguettes in half lengthwise. Divide the cooked pork between the 4 baguettes. Top with 2 sliced tomatoes and a small handful of fresh mint and cilantro leaves. Top with the baguette lids, cut each baguette in half, and serve. **Total cooking time 10 minutes.**

66

# creamy pork, apple & mustard

Serves **4**

Total cooking time **20 minutes**

2 tablespoons **olive oil**

2 tablespoons **butter**

1 large **red onion**, cut into slim wedges

2 medium **red apples**, cored and cut into slim wedges

1 lb 5 oz **pork tenderloin**, thinly sliced

1¼ cups hot **chicken stock**

¾ cup **sour cream**

2 tablespoons **Dijon mustard**

2 tablespoons **whole-grain mustard**

6 tablespoons chopped **parsley**

**mashed potatoes**, to serve

**Heat** the oil and butter in a large skillet, add the onion and apples and cook over medium-high heat for 5 minutes, turning and stirring occasionally, until golden and starting to soften. Remove with a slotted spoon and keep warm.

**Add** the pork to the pan and cook over high heat for 5 minutes until golden and cooked through. Return the onion and apples to the pan with the stock and bring to a boil. Reduce the heat and simmer for 3 minutes, until the stock has reduced by half, then add the sour cream and mustards and heat through for 2 minutes.

**Stir** in the parsley, then serve hot with mashed potatoes.

**For simple pork, apple & mustard pan-fry,** heat 2 tablespoons olive oil and 2 tablespoons butter in a large skillet, add 1 large cored and coarsely chopped apple and 1 lb 5 oz thinly sliced pork tenderloin and cook for 5 minutes, stirring occasionally, until golden and cooked through. Stir in ¾ cup sour cream and 2 tablespoons whole-grain mustard until well combined. Sprinkle with 2 tablespoons chopped parsley and serve with ready-cooked rice or mashed potatoes. **Total cooking time 10 minutes.**

# beef & potato balti with spinach

Serves **4**
Total cooking time **30 minutes**

3 tablespoons **vegetable oil**
14½ oz **stir-fry beef strips**
1 **red bell pepper**, cored,
    seeded, and cut into
    large chunks
1 **onion**, thickly sliced
1½ cups diced **sweet potato**
2 cups **balti cooking sauce**
3 **tomatoes**, cut into wedges
4 cups **spinach**, washed and
    coarsely chopped

**Heat** 2 tablespoons of the oil in a sauté pan set over medium-high heat and cook the beef for 3–4 minutes, stirring occasionally, until browned and just cooked through. Remove from the pan with a slotted spoon and set aside. Return the pan to the heat.

**Add** the remaining oil to the pan and cook the bell pepper, onion, and sweet potato for 5–6 minutes, stirring frequently, until lightly colored and softened.

**Stir** the balti sauce into the pan with the tomato wedges, then reduce the heat, cover, and simmer gently for about 15 minutes or until the vegetables are tender and the sauce has thickened slightly.

**Return** the beef to the pan, add the spinach and stir over the heat for 1–2 minutes, until the beef is hot and the spinach has wilted. Serve immediately.

**For curried beef stir-fry with spinach**, heat 2 tablespoons oil in a skillet and cook 14½ oz stir-fry beef strips over high heat for 2 minutes, until browned all over. Add 1 thinly sliced onion and cook for 2 minutes. Reduce the heat, stir in 2 tablespoons Madras or balti curry paste, and cook for 1 minute. Pour in 1⅔ cups reduced-fat coconut milk and ¾ cup hot beef or vegetable stock. Simmer gently for 2 minutes. Stir in 4 cups coarsely chopped spinach until just wilted. Serve with naan bread or rice. **Total cooking time 10 minutes.**

# sausage & bean cassoulet

Serves **4**

Total cooking time **30 minutes**

2 tablespoons **olive oil**

6 **pork sausages**

1 **onion**, chopped

2 **garlic cloves**, chopped

1 (14½ oz) can **diced tomatoes**

½ cup **chicken stock**

1 **bay leaf**

1 (15 oz) can **cannellini beans**, rinsed and drained

1 cup **dried bread crumbs**

handful of chopped **thyme**

**salt** and **pepper**

**Heat** 1 tablespoon of the oil in a shallow, flameproof casserole dish. Add the sausages and cook for 5 minutes until starting to turn golden, then add the onion and cook for another 5 minutes, until softened.

**Cut** the sausages into thick slices, then return to the pan with the garlic and cook for 1 minute. Add the tomatoes, stock, bay leaf, and beans, season with salt and pepper to taste and bring to a boil. Reduce the heat and simmer for 5 minutes.

**Mix** together the bread crumbs and thyme and sprinkle over the cassoulet, then drizzle over the remaining oil. Cook in a preheated oven, 400°F, for 10–12 minutes, until the topping is golden and crisp.

**For creamy white bean & sausage bake**, mix together 4 sliced cooked smoked sausages, 2 (15 oz) cans cannellini beans, rinsed and drained, ½ cup sour cream, 5 tablespoons hot vegetable stock, and a handful of chopped thyme. Pour into an ovenproof dish and top with ¾ cup dried bread crumbs and ¼ cup shredded Gruyère cheese. Place in a preheated oven, 425°F, for 15 minutes, until golden and bubbling. **Total cooking time 20 minutes.**

# sweet & sour pork

Serves **4**

Total cooking time **20 minutes**

1 tablespoon **vegetable oil**

½ **pineapple**, skinned, cored, and cut into bite-size chunks

1 **onion**, cut into chunks

1 **orange bell pepper**, cored, seeded, and cut into chunks

12 oz **pork tenderloin**, cut into strips

3½ oz **snow peas**, halved lengthwise

6 tablespoons **ketchup**

2 tablespoons **packed light brown sugar**

2 tablespoons **white wine** or **malt vinegar**

**egg noodles**, to serve (optional)

**Heat** the oil in a large, heavy skillet or wok and stir-fry the pineapple chunks over very high heat for 3–4 minutes, until browned in places. Remove with a slotted spoon. Add the onion and orange pepper and cook over high heat, stirring frequently, for 5 minutes, until softened. Add the pork strips and stir-fry for 5 minutes, until browned and cooked through.

**Return** the pineapple to the pan with the snow peas and cook, stirring occasionally, for 2 minutes. Mix the ketchup, sugar, and vinegar together in a small bowl and pour over the pork mixture. Toss and cook for 1 minute more to heat the sauce through.

**Serve** immediately, with egg noodles, if desired.

**For speedy sweet & sour pork stir-fry**, drain the juice from 1 (14 oz) can crushed pineapple and blend 5 tablespoons of juice with 2 tablespoons cornstarch, add ¼ cup rice vinegar and 2 tablespoons each ketchup, dark soy sauce, and light brown sugar. Heat 1 tablespoon vegetable oil in a large skillet over high heat and stir-fry 7 oz pork strips for 2 minutes. Add 1 cored, seeded, and chopped red bell pepper, stir-fry for 2 minutes, then add 5 shredded scallions, the pineapple, and the pineapple juice mixture. Warm through and serve with noodles. **Total cooking time 10 minutes.**

# chorizo, paprika & bean stew

Serves **4**

Total cooking time **30 minutes**

2 tablespoons **olive oil**

7 oz **bacon lardons**

8 oz **mini cooking Spanish chorizo sausages**

1 **onion**, finely chopped

3 (14½ oz) cans **diced tomatoes with herbs**

1 teaspoon **sugar**

1 tablespoon **sweet smoked paprika**

2 **garlic cloves**, crushed

1 **carrot**, peeled and finely diced

1 **celery stick**, finely diced

1 **bay leaf**

1 **chicken bouillon cube**, crumbled

2 (15 oz) cans **mixed beans**, such as black-eyed peas and red kidney beans, rinsed and drained

¼ cup finely chopped **flat-leaf parsley**, plus extra to garnish

**salt** and **pepper**

**crusty bread**, to serve (optional)

**Heat** the oil in a large, heavy saucepan, add the bacon and chorizo sausages, and cook over high heat for 3–4 minutes, until golden brown.

**Stir** in the onion, tomatoes, sugar, paprika, garlic, carrot, celery, bay leaf, and crumbled bouillon cube, then reduce the heat to medium and cook, uncovered, for 15–20 minutes.

**Add** the beans and bring back to a boil, then cook for 2–3 minutes or until piping hot. Season and stir in the parsley.

**Ladle** into bowls, sprinkle with extra chopped parsley and serve with crusty bread, if desired.

**For quick chorizo, paprika & bean soup**, heat 1 tablespoon olive oil in a large saucepan, add 7 oz diced chorizo and cook over high heat for 2–3 minutes. Stir in 1 teaspoon sweet smoked paprika, then add 2½ cups ready-made fresh tomato soup and 1 (15 oz) can mixed beans, rinsed and drained. Bring to a boil, then reduce the heat to medium and cook for 3–4 minutes or until piping hot. Serve with crusty bread. **Total cooking time 10 minutes.**

# cowboy beef & bean casserole

Serves **4**

Total cooking time **30 minutes**

2 tablespoons **olive oil**

1 **onion**, chopped

2 **garlic cloves**, chopped

14½ oz **beef**, cut into strips

1½ tablespoons **chipotle paste**

1 teaspoon **ground cumin**

1½ teaspoons **sweet smoked paprika**

6 oz **smoked pork sausage**, thickly sliced

1 cup **lager**

1 (14½ oz) can **diced tomatoes**

2 tablespoons **tomato paste**

1 (15 oz) can **beans** (red or white kidney), rinsed and drained

1 **roasted red pepper** from a jar, drained and sliced (optional)

**Tabasco** or **other hot sauce**

**salt** and **pepper**

**To serve**

**steamed rice**

**sour cream**

**Heat** the oil in a large saucepan or flameproof casserole dish. Add the onion and garlic and cook for 6–7 minutes, stirring frequently, to soften.

**Meanwhile,** toss the beef strips in the chipotle paste, cumin, and paprika. Add the beef and sausage to the onion mixture and stir over medium heat for 1 minute. Add the lager, tomatoes, tomato paste, beans, roasted pepper (if using), and a few shakes of Tabasco. Season, then cover and simmer over medium-low heat for about 20 minutes or until rich and thick.

**Ladle** into dishes and serve with steamed rice and a dollop of sour cream.

**For cowboy bean stew**, heat 2 tablespoons oil in a skillet over medium-high heat. Mix 1 lb 7 oz beef stir-fry strips with the chipotle paste and spices, as above, and stir-fry for 5–6 minutes, until the meat is browned. Add 2 (16 oz) cans baked beans, heated, 1 tablespoon Worcestershire sauce, and a few shakes of Tabasco. Serve with baked potatoes or steamed rice and a dollop of sour cream, as above. **Total cooking time 10 minutes.**

# bacon, tomato & bean salad

Serves **4**
Total cooking time **10 minutes**

3 tablespoons **olive** or
   **vegetable oil**
6 **Canadian bacon slices**,
   chopped
2 **garlic cloves**, chopped
1 teaspoon **paprika**
3 **tomatoes**, seeded and
   diced
2 (15 oz) cans **lima beans**,
   rinsed and drained
2 tablespoons chopped
   **parsley**
2 tablespoons **lemon juice**

**Heat** the oil in a large skillet and cook the bacon over medium heat for 6–7 minutes, stirring occasionally, until crisp and golden. Stir in the garlic and paprika for the final minute of cooking, then add the tomatoes, lima beans, parsley, and lemon juice and toss to warm through.

**Spoon** into 4 dishes and serve immediately.

**For tomato, bacon & lima bean stew**, heat 3 tablespoons olive or vegetable oil in a large saucepan and cook 6 slices of coarsely chopped Canadian bacon over medium heat for 4–5 minutes, until golden, then add 1 chopped onion and cook for another 4–5 minutes, until softened. Stir 2 large carrots, peeled and diced, 2 chopped garlic cloves, and 1 teaspoon paprika into the pan and cook for 1–2 minutes, until the garlic is softened. Add 1 (15 oz) can lima beans, rinsed and drained, 1 (14½ oz) can diced tomatoes, and 1 cup hot vegetable stock. Bring to a boil, then cover, reduce the heat, and simmer gently for about 15 minutes, until thickened. Sprinkle with 2 tablespoons chopped fresh cilantro and serve with couscous. **Total cooking time 30 minutes.**

# beef, pumpkin & prune stew

Serves **4**

Total cooking time **30 minutes**

2 tablespoons **olive oil**

1 **garlic clove**, chopped

1 large **onion**, chopped

1 lb peeled, seeded, and
cubed **pumpkin**

1 lb 5 oz **beef steak** (such as
sirloin, porterhouse, or flank),
cubed

2 teaspoons **ground
coriander**

2 teaspoons **ground cumin**

1 cup **ready-to-eat soft
dried prunes**

2 (14½ oz) cans **diced
tomatoes**

1¾ cups hot **beef stock**

3 cups **fresh cilantro**,
chopped

**To serve**
**couscous**
**plain yogurt**

**Heat** the oil in a large saucepan or flameproof
casserole, add the garlic, onion, pumpkin, and beef and
cook over high heat for 5–10 minutes, until the beef is
browned and the pumpkin is golden. Add the spices
and cook for another 1 minute.

**Add** the prunes, tomatoes, and stock and bring to a boil,
then reduce the heat, cover, and simmer for 15 minutes,
stirring occasionally, until the stew is thickened and the
meat and vegetables are cooked through.

**Sprinkle** with the chopped cilantro and stir through.
Serve with couscous, topped with spoonfuls of yogurt.

**For speedy beef, tomato & prune pan-fry**, heat
2 tablespoons olive oil in a large skillet, add 1 lb 5 oz
thinly sliced flank steak and cook over high heat for
2 minutes. Add 2 teaspoons ground coriander,
2 teaspoons ground cumin, and 8 chopped tomatoes
and cook for another 2–3 minutes, until softened.
Serve hot, topped with 12 coarsely chopped ready-
to-eat dried prunes and 2 tablespoons chopped fresh
cilantro. **Total cooking time 10 minutes.**

# roast pork with fennel & lemon

Serves **4**

Total cooking time **30 minutes**

2 (12 oz) **pork tenderloins**
2 tablespoons **olive oil**
2 **lemons**
1½ lb small **new potatoes**,
  halved
1 **fennel bulb**, sliced
3–4 **sage leaves**
**salt** and **pepper**

**Rub** the pork with a little of the oil and place in a large, shallow roasting pan. Finely grate the peel of 1 lemon and sprinkle over the pork with salt and lots of pepper.

**Spread** the potatoes around the pork and drizzle over the remaining oil. Place in a preheated oven, 425°F, for 10 minutes.

**Cut** the other lemon into wedges and add to the roasting pan with the fennel and sage leaves. Return to the oven for 15 minutes, until the meat and potatoes are cooked through.

**For fennel & lemon porkballs with cannellini beans**, mix 13 oz ground pork with the finely grated zest of 1 lemon, 1 teaspoon crushed fennel seeds, ½ finely chopped red chile, 1 cup fresh white bread crumbs, and 1 egg yolk. Season to taste and use wet hands to shape into 12 balls. Heat 1 tablespoon olive oil in a flameproof casserole dish. Sauté the balls for 5 minutes, until golden, then add 1 cup hot chicken stock and simmer for 5 minutes. Add 4 oz halved cherry tomatoes and 1 (15 oz) can cannellini beans, rinsed and drained. Cook for another 5 minutes, until heated through, then serve sprinkled with chopped basil. **Total cooking time 20 minutes.**

# eggs with merguez sausage

Serves **4**

Total cooking time **20 minutes**

2 tablespoons **olive oil**

1 **onion**, finely sliced

1 **red chile**, seeded and finely chopped

1 **garlic clove**, crushed

10 oz **merguez sausages**, coarsely chopped

1 teaspoon **dried oregano**

1 (14½ oz) can **cherry tomatoes**

6 tablespoons **tomato puree** or **tomato sauce with herbs**

1 cup **roasted mixed peppers** from a jar, drained and coarsely chopped

4 **eggs**

**salt** and **pepper**

¼ cup finely chopped **fresh cilantro**, to garnish

**Heat** the oil in a large skillet, add the onion, red chile, garlic, merguez sausages, and oregano and cook gently for about 5 minutes or until the onion is softened. Add the tomatoes, tomato puree or sauce, and peppers and cook for another 5 minutes. If the sauce looks dry, add a splash of water.

**Season** well, then make 4 hollows in the mixture, break an egg into each and cover the pan. Cook for 5 minutes or until the eggs are set.

**Divide** among 4 serving plates, sprinkle with chopped cilantro, and serve immediately.

### For Merguez sausage & tomato tortilla, heat

2 tablespoons sunflower oil in a medium ovenproof skillet, add 1 chopped onion, 7 oz coarsely chopped merguez sausages, 1 seeded and chopped red chile, and 1 chopped garlic clove and cook over medium heat for 3–4 minutes. Add 2 chopped tomatoes and cook for another 3–4 minutes. Lightly beat 6 eggs in a bowl, then season with salt and pepper and pour into the pan. Cook over medium heat for 10–12 minutes or until the base is set, then place the pan under a preheated medium-hot broiler and cook for 4–5 minutes or until the top is golden and set. Cut the tortilla into wedges and serve. **Total cooking time 30 minutes.**

# bacon, pea & zucchini risotto

Serves **4**

Total cooking time **30 minutes**

3½ tablespoons **butter**

5 oz **bacon**, diced

1½ cups **risotto rice**

6 tablespoons **dry white wine** (optional)

4 cups hot **chicken** or **vegetable stock** (add an extra 6 tablespoons if not using wine)

2 **zucchini**, about 11 oz total weight, coarsely shredded

1⅓ cups **frozen peas**, defrosted

1 small bunch of **basil**, shredded (optional)

**salt** and **pepper**

grated **Parmesan cheese**, to serve

**Melt** the butter in a large skillet or saucepan and cook the diced bacon over medium heat for 6–7 minutes, until golden. Remove half of the bacon with a slotted spoon and set aside.

**Stir** in the risotto rice and pour in the white wine, if using, and hot stock. Bring to a boil, then simmer gently for 15–18 minutes, stirring as often as possible, until the rice is tender and creamy. Stir in the shredded zucchini and defrosted peas for the final 2–3 minutes of cooking time.

**Season,** then spoon the risotto into 4 bowls. Top with the reserved bacon and shredded basil, if using. Serve sprinkled with grated Parmesan cheese.

**For lazy pea & bacon noodles**, heat 3½ tablespoons butter in a large saucepan and cook 7 oz finely chopped bacon over medium-high heat, stirring occasionally, for 4–5 minutes, until lightly golden. Pour over 2½ cups boiling ham, chicken, or vegetable stock, 2 tablespoons barbecue sauce, 1⅓ cups frozen peas, and 13 oz fresh noodles. Cover and simmer for 3–4 minutes, until the peas and noodles are tender. Lift out the noodles and heap into bowls, then pour over the soup to serve. **Total cooking time 10 minutes.**

# spicy beef & squash stew

Serves **4**

Total cooking time **30 minutes**

2 tablespoons **vegetable oil**
2 large **beef steaks**, cut into
  chunks
1 **onion**, finely chopped
1 small **butternut squash**,
  peeled and cut into chunks
1 **red chile**, seeded and
  chopped
1 teaspoon **ground cumin**
1 tablespoon **tomato paste**
1 (14½ oz) can **cherry
  tomatoes**
⅔ cup **canned corn kernels**
handful of chopped **fresh
  cilantro**, to garnish

**Heat** half the oil in a large, heavy saucepan. Add the steak and cook over high heat for about 3 minutes, until browned, then remove from the pan and set aside.

**Add** the remaining oil to the pan with the onion and squash and cook for 5 minutes, until softened. Stir in the chile and cumin and cook for 30 seconds, then add the tomato paste and tomatoes and simmer for 15 minutes.

**Return** the beef to the pan with the corn kernels and heat through. Serve sprinkled with the cilantro.

**For beef, tomato & beans with nacho topping**, heat 1 tablespoon oil in a large, flameproof skillet. Add 1 finely chopped onion and cook for 2 minutes, then stir in 10 oz ground beef. Cook for 5 minutes, until golden, then add 1 teaspoon each of ground coriander and cumin. Stir in ¾ cup canned diced tomatoes and simmer for 10 minutes, topping up with a little water if necessary. Add ¾ cup canned kidney beans, rinsed and drained, and heat through. Arrange 3 oz tortilla chips on top of the stew and sprinkle with ½ cup shredded cheddar cheese. Cook under a preheated hot broiler for 1–2 minutes, until the cheese melts. Serve with sour cream, guacamole, and salsa. **Total cooking time 20 minutes.**

# caramelized parsnips

Serves **2**

Total cooking time **20 minutes**

1¼ lb **parsnips**, scrubbed or
  peeled
3½ tablespoons **butter**
6 oz diced **bacon**
3 tablespoons **sugar**
⅓ cup **pine nuts**
5 tablespoons chopped **thyme
  leaves**

**Cut** the parsnips in half widthwise, then cut the
chunky tops into quarters lengthwise and the slim
bottom halves in half lengthwise.

**Heat** the butter in a large wok or skillet, add the
bacon and parsnips, and cook over medium heat for
15 minutes, turning and tossing occasionally, until
the parsnips are golden and softened and the bacon
is crisp.

**Add** the sugar and pine nuts and cook for 2–3
minutes more, until lightly caramelized. Toss with
the thyme and serve.

**For bacon, pine nut & parsnip rosti**, shred 11½ oz
peeled parsnips into a bowl and mix with 2 oz ready-
cooked bacon slices, snipped into small pieces, and
2 tablespoons chopped parsley. Divide the mixture
and squeeze together to form 4 balls, then flatten into
patties. Heat 3½ tablespoons butter in a large skillet,
add the patties, and cook over high heat for 2 minutes
on each side until golden. Serve hot with a green salad
and sprinkled with pine nuts. **Total cooking time
10 minutes.**

# spicy lamb & vegetable stew

Serves **4**

Total cooking time **30 minutes**

1 tablespoon **sunflower oil**
1 lb 5 oz **boneless lamb neck**, cut into ¾ inch cubes
1 **onion**, chopped
1 **garlic clove**, crushed
1 teaspoon peeled and grated **fresh ginger root**
2 tablespoons **medium curry paste**
1 large **potato**, peeled and cut into ¾ inch cubes
1 large **carrot**, peeled and cut into ¾ inch cubes
1⅔ cups hot **lamb stock**
¾ cup **coconut milk**
1⅓ cups **frozen peas**
handful of chopped **fresh cilantro**, to garnish
steamed **rice**, to serve (optional)

**Heat** the oil in a large, heavy saucepan, add the lamb, onion, garlic, and ginger and cook over high heat for 3–4 minutes, stirring frequently, until the lamb is browned and the onion is softened. Reduce the heat to medium, add the curry paste, and cook, stirring, for another 1–2 minutes.

**Stir** in the potato, carrot, stock, and coconut milk and bring to a boil. Cook, uncovered, for 15–20 minutes or until the lamb and vegetables are tender. Stir in the peas 3 minutes before the end of the cooking time.

**Ladle** into bowls, sprinkle with the cilantro, and serve with steamed rice, if desired.

**For spicy lamb & vegetable curry**, heat 2 tablespoons sunflower oil in a large wok or skillet until hot. Add 1 chopped onion, 2 chopped garlic cloves, and 1 teaspoon peeled and grated fresh ginger root and stir-fry over high heat for 1–2 minutes, then add 1 lb 5 oz ground lamb, 3 tablespoons medium curry paste, 1⅓ cups each diced potatoes and carrots, and stir-fry for another 1–2 minutes, until the lamb is browned. Pour in ¾ cup coconut milk and cook, uncovered, over medium heat for 10–12 minutes, stirring frequently, until the lamb and vegetables are tender. Season with salt and pepper, then serve immediately with steamed rice or crusty bread. **Total cooking time 20 minutes.**

# west indian beef & bean stew

Serves **4**
Total cooking time **30 minutes**

3 tablespoons **sunflower oil**
1¾ lb **ground beef**
6 whole **cloves**
1 **onion**, finely chopped
2 tablespoons **medium curry powder**
2 **carrots**, peeled and cut into ½ inch cubes
2 **celery sticks**, diced
1 tablespoon **thyme** leaves
2 **garlic cloves**, crushed
¼ cup **tomato paste**
2½ cups hot **beef stock**
1 large **potato**, peeled and cut into ½ inch cubes
1 (7 oz) can **black beans**, rinsed and drained
1 (7 oz) can **black-eyed peas**, rinsed and drained
**salt** and **pepper**
**lemon** wedges, to serve

**Heat** the oil in a large, heavy saucepan, add the beef and fry, stirring, over medium-high heat for 5–6 minutes or until browned.

**Add** the cloves, onion, and curry powder and cook for 2–3 minutes, until the onions are beginning to soften, then stir in the carrots, celery, thyme, garlic, and tomato paste.

**Pour** in the beef stock to just cover the meat and stir well, then add the potato and beans and bring to a boil. Reduce the heat slightly and simmer for 20 minutes, uncovered, or until the potatoes and beef are tender, then season with salt and pepper to taste.

**Ladle** into bowls and serve with lemon wedges.

**For curried beef & black bean pilau**, heat 2 tablespoons sunflower oil in a large wok or skillet until hot, add 1 lb ground beef and 1 tablespoon medium curry paste and stir-fry over high heat for 2–3 minutes, until browned. Add 6 tablespoons coconut milk, reduce the heat to medium, and simmer gently for 6–8 minutes or until most of the liquid has been absorbed and the beef is cooked through. Stir in 3½ cups ready-cooked long-grain or basmati rice and 1 (7 oz) can black beans, rinsed and drained, and heat through for 2–3 minutes or until piping hot. Season, then serve immediately. **Total cooking time 20 minutes.**

# pork & paprika goulash

Serves **4**

Total cooking time **30 minutes**

2 tablespoons **vegetable oil**

13 oz **boneless pork loin**, cubed

1 **onion**, sliced

2 teaspoons **smoked paprika**

1 (14½ oz) can **diced tomatoes**

1 lb **potatoes**, peeled and diced

¼ cup **sour cream**

**salt** and **pepper**

handful of chopped **parsley**, to garnish

**Heat** half the oil in a deep skillet. Add the pork, season with salt and pepper to taste and cook for 5 minutes, until browned all over. Remove from the pan and set aside. Add the remaining oil to the pan along with the onion and cook for 5 minutes, until softened.

**Stir** in the paprika, then add the tomatoes and potatoes. Season to taste, bring to a boil, then reduce the heat and simmer for 10 minutes.

**Return** the pork to the pan and cook for another 5 minutes, until the pork and potatoes are cooked through. Divide among serving bowls, top with the sour cream, and serve sprinkled with parsley.

**For crispy paprika pork chops with roasted peppers**, mix ¾ cup dried bread crumbs with the finely grated zest of ½ lemon and 2 teaspoons smoked paprika. Dip 4 pork chops into olive oil, then press into the bread-crumb mixture and season to taste. Arrange the chops on a baking sheet with 2 cored, seeded, and sliced red bell peppers. Place in a preheated oven, 425°F, for 15 minutes, until the pork is cooked through, then serve with a green salad. **Total cooking time 20 minutes.**

# fish &
# seafood

# crispy fish pie

Serves **4**

Total cooking time **30 minutes**

**butter**, for greasing

¾ cup **frozen spinach**

13 oz **skinless salmon fillet**, cubed

8 oz **skinless smoked haddock fillet**, cubed

4 **eggs**

6 tablespoons **sour cream**

2 tablespoons **boiling water**

½ cup **dried bread crumbs**

**salt** and **pepper**

**Lightly** grease an ovenproof dish. Place the spinach in a strainer and pour over boiling water from the kettle until it has defrosted. Lay the spinach on a sheet of kitchen towel and squeeze to get rid of excess water.

**Arrange** the spinach in the ovenproof dish and place the fish on top. Make 4 small holes between the fish pieces and crack an egg into each one.

**Mix** the sour cream with the measured water and season with salt and pepper to taste. Pour over the fish, then sprinkle with the bread crumbs. Place in a preheated oven, 400°F, for 25 minutes or until golden and bubbling and the fish is cooked through.

**For fish pots with crispy topping**, divide 8 oz skinless smoked haddock fillet, cut into small pieces, between 4 ramekins. Stir together ⅓ cup sour cream, a handful of chopped chives, and 2 tablespoons water, then stir into the fish. Place in a preheated oven, 350°F, for 5–7 minutes. Crack an egg on top of each ramekin, top with a sprinkling of dried bread crumbs and a drizzle of melted butter, then return to the oven for 10–12 minutes more, until the eggs are set. Serve with crusty bread. **Total cooking time 20 minutes.**

# rich tomato, wine & fish stew

Serves **4**

Total cooking time **10 minutes**

2 (13 oz) jars **tomato sauce with peppers and onion**

⅔ cup **white wine**

1 tablespoon **olive oil**

12 oz **skinless white fish fillets**, torn or cut into chunks

6 oz **raw peeled shrimp**

½ cup **parsley**, chopped

**pepper**

**crusty bread**, to serve (optional)

**Place** the tomato sauce, wine, and oil in a large, heavy saucepan and bring to a boil.

**Reduce** the heat, add the fish and shrimp, and simmer for 7 minutes, until the fish is opaque and cooked through and the shrimp have turned pink.

**Add** the parsley and season with pepper, then serve in bowls with warm crusty bread, if desired.

**For Mediterranean fish stew with chunky vegetables**, heat 1 tablespoon olive oil in a large, deep skillet and cook 2 trimmed and chunkily chopped zucchini, 1 pointed sweet red pepper and 1 yellow bell pepper, each cored, seeded, and cut into chunks, and 1 finely chopped red onion over medium heat, stirring occasionally, for 8–10 minutes, until softened. Add 1 lb mixed skinless white fish fillets, cut into chunks, 6 oz cooked peeled shrimp, 2 (13 oz) jars tomato pasta sauce, and 1¼ cups white wine and cook, stirring very gently occasionally, for 10 minutes or until the fish is cooked through. Stir in ½ cup pitted black ripe olives and serve in bowls topped with ½ cup ready-made croûtons. **Total cooking time 30 minutes.**

# smoked haddock kedgeree

Serves **4**

Total cooking time **30 minutes**

1 tablespoon **vegetable oil**

2 tablespoons **butter**

1 **onion**, finely chopped

1 **garlic clove**, crushed

1 teaspoon finely grated **fresh ginger root**

1 teaspoon **cumin seeds**

½ teaspoon **coriander seeds**

1 teaspoon **curry powder**

½ teaspoon **ground turmeric**

1½ cups **basmati rice**

2¾ cups hot **chicken** or **fish stock**

10 oz **skinless smoked haddock fillet**

½ cup **frozen peas**

1 **red chile**, seeded, and chopped

handful of chopped **fresh cilantro**

**salt** and **pepper**

**mango chutney**, to serve

**Heat** the oil and butter in a large saucepan. Add the onion and cook for 5 minutes, then stir in the garlic and ginger and cook for 1 minute. Add the cumin and coriander seeds and cook for 30 seconds, then stir in the curry powder, turmeric, and rice and cook for another 1 minute.

**Pour** in the stock and cook for 5 minutes. Place the fish fillet on top of the rice and cook for another 5 minutes. By this time, most of the stock should have boiled away. Add the peas, cover the pan tightly with a lid, turn down the heat as low as it will go and cook for 5–7 minutes, until the rice is cooked through.

**Use** a fork to gently break up the fish, stir the fish and peas into the rice, and season with salt and pepper to taste. Sprinkle with the chile and cilantro and serve with mango chutney.

**For smoked haddock, rice & spinach soup**, cook 1 chopped onion in 1 tablespoon oil for 5 minutes, then add ½ cup basmati rice, 6 cups hot chicken or fish stock, and a pinch of saffron threads. Simmer for 10 minutes, then add 10 oz skinless smoked haddock fillet and cook for 3 minutes, until starting to break up. Add 6 tablespoons light cream and 2 cups baby spinach leaves and heat through until wilted. **Total cooking time 20 minutes.**

# clam, kale & lima bean stew

Serves **4**

Total cooking time **20 minutes**

1 tablespoon **olive oil**

2 oz **chorizo**, chopped

1 **onion**, finely chopped

2 **garlic cloves**, chopped

1 teaspoon **tomato paste**

3 tablespoons **dry white wine**

¾ cup hot **chicken stock**

1 cup chopped **kale**

1 lb **clams**, rinsed and drained

1 (8½ oz) can **lima beans**, rinsed and drained

**salt** and **pepper**

**Heat** the oil in a large saucepan or flameproof casserole dish. Add the chorizo and cook for 1 minute, until starting to release its oil. Add the onion and cook for another 5 minutes, until softened, then stir in the garlic and tomato paste and cook for 1 minute.

**Pour** in the wine and let it bubble away until reduced by half. Add the stock and kale and cook for 5 minutes.

**Add** the clams, cover, and cook for 3 minutes, then stir in the beans. Cover and cook for another 3 minutes, until the clams have opened, discarding any that have not. Season with salt and pepper to taste and serve.

**For stir-fried clams & kale in black bean sauce**, heat 2 tablespoons oil in a wok. Add 2 sliced garlic cloves and cook for a few seconds, then add 2 cups chopped kale and stir-fry for 1–2 minutes. Add ½ finely chopped chile and 2 teaspoons finely grated fresh ginger root and stir in, then add 1 lb clams, rinsed and drained, and ⅓ cup black bean sauce. Add a splash of water, cover and cook for 5 minutes, until the clams have opened, discarding any that have not. Sprinkle with 1 sliced scallion before serving with ready-cooked rice. **Total cooking time 10 minutes.**

# creamy, curried mussel soup

Serves **4**

Total cooking time **20 minutes**

1 tablespoon **butter**

2 **shallots**, thinly sliced

2 **garlic cloves**, crushed

1 teaspoon peeled and finely grated **fresh ginger root**

2 large **red chiles**, seeded and finely diced

1 teaspoon **medium curry powder**

1 large pinch of **saffron threads**

6 tablespoons **dry white wine**

1⅔ cups hot **vegetable stock**

2¼ lb **live mussels**, scrubbed and debearded

¾ cup **heavy cream**

6 tablespoons finely chopped **fresh cilantro**

**salt** and **pepper**

**crusty bread**, to serve (optional)

**Heat** the butter in a large wok or skillet, add the shallots, garlic, ginger, red chiles, and curry powder and stir-fry over high heat for 1 minute. Add the saffron, white wine, and stock and bring to a boil, then reduce the heat to medium and cook for 1–2 minutes.

**Add** the mussels to the pan, discarding any that are cracked or don't shut when tapped, and cover tightly. Increase the heat to high and cook for 2–3 minutes, shaking the pan occasionally, until the mussels have opened. Discard any that remain closed. Remove the mussels with a slotted spoon and set aside.

**Pour** the cream into the stock mixture and bring back to a boil, then reduce the heat and simmer gently, uncovered, for 5–6 minutes. Return the mussels to the pan, stir in the cilantro, and season to taste.

**Ladle** into soup bowls and serve with crusty bread, if desired.

**For curried smoked mussel omelet**, beat together 4 eggs and 2 teaspoons hot curry powder in a bowl, then season with salt. Heat 2 tablespoons butter in a large skillet and add the egg mixture, swirling to coat evenly. Cook for 1–2 minutes and then add a drained 3 oz can smoked mussels in olive oil down the center. Fold the egg mixture over the mussels. Flip to seal and cook for 1–2 minutes. Keep warm while you repeat the recipe, to make 2 omelets in total. Divide each omelet in two and serve one half per person. **Total cooking time 10 minutes.**

# baked tuna with ratatouille

Serves **4**

Total cooking time **30 minutes**

1 **onion**, cut into wedges
1 **eggplant**, cut into chunks
1 **red bell pepper**, cored,
  seeded, and cut into chunks
1 **zucchini**, thickly sliced
4 **tomatoes**, quartered
5 tablespoons **olive oil**
2 **garlic cloves**, crushed
1 tablespoon **sherry vinegar**
4 **tuna steaks**
**salt** and **pepper**
handful of chopped **basil**, to
  garnish

**Toss** the vegetables with 3 tablespoons of the oil, arrange in a shallow roasting dish and season with salt and pepper to taste. Place in a preheated oven, 400°F, for 15 minutes, turning occasionally, until lightly charred.

**Mix** the remaining oil with the garlic and vinegar and stir into the vegetables. Arrange the tuna steaks in the dish and season well. Return to the oven for another 12–15 minutes, until the tuna is cooked. Serve immediately, sprinkled with the basil.

### For roasted tuna with ratatouille topping, rub

1 tablespoon olive oil over 4 tuna steaks and place in a shallow roasting pan. Place 3 oz halved cherry tomatoes, 1 cored, seeded, and chopped red bell pepper, 1 sliced garlic clove, and 1 tablespoon capers, rinsed and drained, over the fish, season well, and drizzle over 1 tablespoon olive oil. Place in a preheated oven, 400°F, for 12–15 minutes, until the vegetables are lightly charred and the tuna is cooked. Sprinkle with chopped basil before serving with crusty bread. **Total cooking time 20 minutes.**

# salmon, pea & dill tortilla

Serves **4**
Total cooking time **30 minutes**

13 oz **potatoes**, peeled and
   thickly sliced
5 oz **skinless salmon fillet**
6 **eggs**, beaten
handful of **dill weed**, chopped
⅔ cup **frozen peas**
1 **scallion**, sliced
1 tablespoon **vegetable oil**
**salt** and **pepper**
**mixed salad greens**, to serve

**Cook** the potatoes in a saucepan of lightly salted boiling water for 10 minutes, until tender, then drain.

**Meanwhile,** place the salmon in a small saucepan. Cover with boiling water and let simmer for 7 minutes, until the fish flakes easily. Drain, then break into large flakes.

**Mix** together the eggs, dill, peas, and scallion, then season with salt and pepper. Heat the oil in an 8 inch nonstick skillet. Stir the potatoes and salmon into the egg mixture, then tip into the pan. Cook over very low heat for 10–15 minutes, until just set. Cut into wedges and serve with mixed salad greens.

**For pea & salmon omelets**, cook 3 tablespoons frozen peas in boiling water for 3 minutes, until cooked through, then drain. Beat 4 eggs together with some dill. Heat 1 tablespoon butter in a small skillet. Add a quarter of the egg mixture and swirl around the pan. Cook for 1 minute, until the mixture is starting to set, then sprinkle with 1 teaspoon grated Parmesan cheese, a few of the peas, and a slice of smoked salmon, cut into strips. Fold over the omelet and keep warm while you repeat with the remaining egg mixture to make 4 omelets in total. **Total cooking time 10 minutes.**

# jumbo shrimp & sweet potato curry

Serves **4**

Total cooking time **30 minutes**

2 tablespoons **vegetable oil**

1 large **onion**, chopped

2 **garlic cloves**, sliced

1 tablespoon peeled and chopped **fresh ginger root**

1 **green chile**, seeded and thinly sliced

3 tablespoons **mild curry paste**

2½ cups diced **sweet potato**

1⅔ cups **coconut milk**

1 cup **vegetable stock**

small handful of **curry leaves**

13 oz **raw peeled jumbo shrimp**

½ cup **frozen leaf spinach**, defrosted and drained

handful of chopped **fresh cilantro**

warm **naan bread**, to serve

**Heat** the oil in a large, deep-sided skillet or wok and cook the onion over medium-high heat for 3–4 minutes, until beginning to color. Add the garlic, ginger, and chile and stir-fry for another 2 minutes. Reduce the heat slightly and add the curry paste, stirring for 1–2 minutes.

**Add** the sweet potato dice, tossing them to coat, then add the coconut milk, stock, and curry leaves. Simmer gently for 12–15 minutes, until the sweet potato is almost tender.

**Stir** the shrimp and spinach into the curry and heat for 2–3 minutes, until the shrimp are just cooked through and pink.

**Sprinkle** with the chopped cilantro, spoon the curry into dishes, and serve immediately with naan bread.

**For curried shrimp broth**, heat 2 tablespoons oil in a large saucepan and fry 2 sliced banana shallots and 2 sliced garlic cloves over high heat, stirring, for 2–3 minutes. Reduce the heat, add 1 tablespoon korma curry paste and stir for 1 minute. Pour 4 cups hot vegetable stock into the pan. Add 10 oz raw peeled jumbo shrimp, 2 cups cooked long-grain rice, 2 seeded and diced tomatoes, and 2 tablespoons chopped cilantro. Simmer for 2–3 minutes, until the shrimp are cooked through, then ladle into bowls to serve. **Total cooking time 10 minutes.**

# rich tomato & fish stew

Serves **4**

Total cooking time **20 minutes**

1 tablespoon **olive oil**

1 **onion**, thinly sliced

1 **garlic clove**, chopped

2 **tomatoes**, coarsely chopped

1 (14½ oz) can **diced tomatoes**

¼ cup **tomato paste**

⅔ cup **white wine**

12 oz **mixed skinless fish fillets**, cut into chunks

6 oz **raw peeled shrimp**

5 tablespoons chopped **thyme**

½ cup **pitted black ripe olives**

**pepper**

warm **crusty bread**, to serve

**Heat** the oil in a large, heavy saucepan and cook the onion and garlic over medium heat, stirring frequently, for 3–4 minutes until softened. Add the fresh tomatoes and cook, stirring, for 2–3 minutes, then add the canned tomatoes, tomato paste, and wine. Bring to a boil and cook over high heat for 5 minutes, until the sauce is thick.

**Stir** the fish chunks and shrimp into the tomato mixture, then reduce the heat, cover, and simmer for 7–8 minutes until the fish is opaque and cooked through and the shrimp have turned pink. Stir through the thyme and black olives and season with pepper to taste.

**Serve** in serving bowls with warm crusty bread to mop up the juices.

**For instant fish stew**, heat 1 tablespoon olive oil in a heavy saucepan and cook 1 finely chopped onion with a squeeze of garlic paste over medium heat, stirring, for 3 minutes. Add 1 (14 oz) can lobster bisque, ½ (14½ oz) can diced tomatoes, 6 oz mixed skinless fish fillets, cut into chunks, and 6 oz cooked peeled shrimp and cook over high heat for 7 minutes until the seafood is cooked through. Serve with crusty bread. **Total cooking time 10 minutes.**

# seafood paella

Serves **4**

Total cooking time **30 minutes**

1 tablespoon **olive oil**

3 oz **chorizo**, thickly sliced

1 **onion**, finely chopped

1 **red bell pepper**, cored,
    seeded, and chopped

2 **garlic cloves**, chopped

1½ cups **paella rice**

1 teaspoon **smoked paprika**

pinch of **saffron threads**

3⅓ cups hot **chicken stock**

10 oz **live mussels**, scrubbed
    and debearded

8 **cooked jumbo shrimp,
    shells on**

3½ oz **raw squid rings**

½ cup **frozen peas**

**salt** and **pepper**

**Heat** the oil in a large, heavy saucepan. Add the chorizo to the pan and cook for about 2 minutes, until starting to brown. Remove from the pan with a slotted spoon and set aside.

**Add** the onion and bell pepper to the pan and cook for 3 minutes, then stir in the garlic and cook for 1 minute. Add the rice and stir until well coated.

**Sprinkle** with the paprika and saffron, return the chorizo to the pan, then pour over the hot stock. Bring to a boil, then simmer, uncovered, for 15 minutes. Add the mussels, cover the pan, and cook for 3 minutes.

**Stir** in the shrimp, squid, and peas and cook for 2 minutes more, until the rice is tender (add a drizzle of hot water around the edge of the pan if still a little firm) and the mussels have opened—discard any that remain closed, then season to taste and serve.

**For saffron & fennel seafood**, heat 2 tablespoons olive oil in a large saucepan. Cook 1 finely chopped fennel bulb for 2 minutes. Add ⅔ cup dry white wine, a good pinch of saffron threads, and 1 lb live mussels, scrubbed and debearded. Cover and cook for 3 minutes. Add 8 cooked peeled large shrimp and 3½ oz raw squid rings. Cook for 2 minutes. Discard any mussels that remain closed. **Total cooking time 10 minutes.**

# angler fish & mixed pepper stew

Serves **4**
Total cooking time **20 minutes**

2 tablespoons **vegetable oil**
2 **onions**, finely chopped
2 tablespoons **medium** or **hot curry powder**
1 teaspoon **ground turmeric**
2 lb **angler fish tail**, cut into bite-size pieces
2 **garlic cloves**, chopped
1 teaspoon peeled and finely grated **fresh ginger root**
½ teaspoon **tamarind paste**
1 tablespoon **thyme leaves**
1 **star anise**
1¾ cups hot **fish stock**
1 **red bell pepper**, cored, seeded, and cut into 1 inch pieces
1 **yellow bell pepper**, cored, seeded, and cut into 1 inch pieces
steamed **rice**, to serve (optional)

**Heat** the oil in a heavy saucepan, add the onions, and cook over medium heat, stirring occasionally, for 2–3 minutes until softened. Stir in the curry powder and turmeric and cook for another 1 minute until fragrant.

**Add** the remaining ingredients and stir together well. Bring to a simmer, then reduce the heat to low and cook, uncovered, for 8–10 minutes or until the fish is cooked through and the peppers are tender.

**Ladle** into bowls and serve with steamed rice, if desired.

### For Chinese angler fish & mixed pepper stir-fry,

core, seed, and finely slice 1 red bell pepper and 1 yellow bell pepper. Heat 2 tablespoons sunflower oil in a large wok or skillet until hot, add the peppers and 1 lb 5 oz angler fish tail, cubed, and stir-fry over high heat for 2–3 minutes. Add ½ cup prepared oyster and scallion stir-fry sauce and fry for another 2–3 minutes or until the fish is cooked through and piping hot. Serve immediately with steamed rice. **Total cooking time 10 minutes.**

# mussels in a coconut broth

Serves **4**

Total cooking time **20 minutes**

1 tablespoon **vegetable oil**

1 **shallot**, finely chopped

1 **garlic clove**, sliced

1 **red chile**, seeded and chopped

2 **lime leaves**, shredded

½ cup **coconut milk**

½ cup **water**

1 **lemon grass stalk**

1 tablespoon **Thai fish sauce**

1 tablespoon **packed brown sugar**

2 lb **live mussels**, scrubbed and debearded

handful of chopped **fresh cilantro**, to serve

**Heat** the oil in a large saucepan, add the shallot and cook for 2 minutes. Stir in the garlic, chile, and lime leaves and cook for 1 minute more. Pour in the coconut milk and the measured water, add the lemon grass, fish sauce, and sugar and let simmer for 10 minutes.

**Add** the mussels, cover, and cook for 3–5 minutes, until the mussels are open, discarding any that remain closed. Sprinkle with the cilantro to serve.

**For spicy wok-roasted mussels**, heat 1 tablespoon vegetable oil in a large wok, add 1 tablespoon Thai green curry paste and cook for 1 minute. Add 2 lb live mussels, scrubbed and debearded, and cook for 1 minute. Pour over 3 tablespoons coconut milk, cover, and cook for 2 minutes more, until the mussels are open, discarding any that remain closed. Sprinkle with 1 chopped scallion, a handful of chopped fresh cilantro and 1 tablespoon lime juice to serve. **Total cooking time 10 minutes.**

# mustard & curry leaf halibut

Serves **4**

Total cooking time **30 minutes**

1 teaspoon **ground turmeric**

1 tablespoon **chili powder**

2 tablespoons grated **fresh coconut**

¼ cup **vegetable oil**

1 teaspoon **black mustard seeds**

20 **fresh curry leaves**

2 **onions**, thinly sliced

4 **green chiles**, seeded and sliced

1 inch piece of **fresh ginger root**, peeled and cut into matchsticks

6 **garlic cloves**, finely chopped

2¼ lb **skinless halibut fillets**, boned and cut into bite-size pieces

1⅔ cups **coconut milk**

1¼ cups **water**

1 tablespoon **tamarind paste**

**salt**

steamed **basmati rice**, to serve (optional)

**Mix** together the turmeric, chili powder, and coconut in a small bowl and set aside.

**Heat** the oil in a large wok or heavy saucepan until hot, then add the mustard seeds and cook over medium-high heat for a few minutes until the seeds begin to pop, then add the curry leaves, onions, green chiles, ginger, and garlic and stir-fry for about 5 minutes, until fragrant.

**Stir** in the turmeric mixture and stir-fry for another 1 minute. Add the fish, then stir in the coconut milk and measured water. Finally, add the tamarind paste. Bring to a boil, then reduce the heat to low and simmer gently, uncovered, for 15 minutes or until the fish is cooked through. Season well with salt.

**Ladle** into bowls and serve with steamed basmati rice, if desired.

### For pan-fried fish with mustard & curry leaves,

mix together 2 tablespoons whole-grain mustard, 6 crushed dried curry leaves, 1 teaspoon chili powder, and 1 teaspoon medium or hot curry powder in a bowl. Season with salt, then spread the mixture all over 4 skinless plaice fillets. Heat 2 tablespoons sunflower oil in a large skillet and fry the fish fillets for 2–3 minutes on each side or until cooked through. Serve with a green salad. **Total cooking time 10 minutes.**

# goan fried fish

Serves **4**

Total cooking time **10 minutes**

1 teaspoon **ground turmeric**
1 teaspoon **ginger paste**
1 teaspoon **garlic paste**
1 teaspoon **chili powder**
1 teaspoon **ground cumin**
1 teaspoon **ground coriander**
juice of 2 **lemons**
4 **skinless halibut steaks**,
  about 7 oz each
¼ cup **sunflower oil**
**salt** and **pepper**
**green salad**, to serve
  (optional)

**Mix** together the ground spices and pastes in a bowl. Add the lemon juice and stir to mix well. Spread the mixture all over the fish and season well with salt and pepper.

**Heat** the sunflower oil in a large skillet, add the fish and fry over medium-high heat for 2–3 minutes on each side or until just cooked through. Serve with a green salad, if desired.

**For Goan fishcakes**, place 13 oz skinless halibut fillets, boned, and 13 oz raw peeled shrimp in a food processor or blender. Add 1 tablespoon Goan curry paste and process until smooth. Using wet hands, shape the mixture into 12 cakes. Heat 2 tablespoons sunflower oil in a large skillet, add the fishcakes, and fry over medium-high heat for 3–4 minutes on each side or until cooked through. Serve with steamed rice and a salad. **Total cooking time 20 minutes.**

# coconut spiced clams

Serves **4**

Total cooking time **20 minutes**

¼ cup **vegetable oil**

2 **shallots**, very finely chopped

1 **red chile**, slit lengthwise and
seeded

1 inch piece of **fresh ginger
root**, peeled and shredded

2 **garlic cloves**, finely chopped

2 **plum tomatoes**, finely
chopped

1 tablespoon **medium** or **hot
curry powder**

¾ cup **coconut milk**

1¾ lb **fresh clams**, scrubbed

large handful of chopped **fresh
cilantro**

3 tablespoons grated **fresh
coconut**

**To serve** (optional)
**salad**
**crusty bread**

**Heat** the oil in a large wok or saucepan until hot, add
the shallots, red chile, ginger, and garlic and stir-fry over
medium heat for 3–4 minutes. Increase the heat to high,
stir in the tomatoes, curry powder, and coconut milk and
cook for another 4–5 minutes.

**Add** the clams to the pan, discarding any that have
cracked or don't shut when tapped, stir to mix and
cover tightly, then continue to cook over high heat for
6–8 minutes, until the clams have opened. Discard any
that remain closed.

**Stir** in the chopped cilantro and sprinkle with the
grated coconut. Ladle into bowls and serve immediately,
with a fresh salad and crusty bread to mop up the juices,
if desired.

### For spicy clam & coconut chowder, heat

2 tablespoons sunflower oil in a heavy saucepan,
add 1 chopped onion, 1 seeded and chopped red chile,
1 tablespoon medium or hot curry powder, and 2 chopped
garlic cloves and cook, stirring, for 2–3 minutes. Add
2½ cups finely diced potatoes, ¾ cup coconut milk, and
2½ cups hot fish stock. Bring to a boil, then reduce the
heat to medium and cook, uncovered, for 12–15 minutes
or until the potatoes are tender. Increase the heat to high,
stir in 13 oz fresh scrubbed clams, discarding any that
are cracked or don't shut when tapped, cover tightly, and
bring to a boil. Cook for 4–5 minutes or until the clams
have opened. Discard any that remain closed. Season
with salt, stir in a small handful of chopped fresh cilantro,
and serve immediately. **Total cooking time 30 minutes.**

# chili seafood stew

Serves **2**

Total cooking time **30 minutes**

2 tablespoons **olive oil**

1 **red onion**, cut into slim wedges

1 small **red chile**, seeded and thinly sliced

1 **garlic clove**, sliced

1½ cups cubed **potatoes**

7 oz **ready-prepared squid rings**

⅔ cup **water**

1 (14½ oz) can **diced tomatoes**

⅔ cup **white wine**

3 tablespoons **tomato paste**

2 tablespoons chopped **sundried tomatoes in oil**, drained

2 tablespoons **thyme leaves**

8 oz **live mussels**, scrubbed and debearded

6 oz **red snapper fillets**, skinned and cut into chunks

**crusty bread**, to serve (optional)

**Heat** the oil in a large skillet, add the onion, chile, and garlic and cook over medium heat for 5–8 minutes, until pale golden and softened. Add the potatoes and squid rings and cook for another 2 minutes.

**Pour** over the measured water, diced tomatoes, wine, and tomato paste and stir well. Add the sundried tomatoes and thyme and cook for 8 minutes.

**Meanwhile,** sort through the mussels, discarding any that don't shut when tapped.

**Add** the red snapper to the pan and stir gently through, then add the mussels, cover, and bring to a boil. Cook for 5–7 minutes, shaking the pan occasionally until the fish is cooked through and the mussels have opened. Discard any that remain closed. Serve with warm crusty bread to mop up the juices, if desired.

**For seafood & chili tomato pan-fry**, heat 1 tablespoon olive oil in a skillet, add 1 small coarsely chopped onion and cook for 2 minutes. Add 1 (14½ oz) can diced tomatoes, ½ teaspoon dried red pepper flakes, ⅔ cup white wine, and a 10 oz pack seafood selection and bring to a boil. Reduce the heat, cover, and simmer for 5 minutes until piping hot. Serve with crusty bread. **Total cooking time 10 minutes.**

# shrimp & mango curry

Serves **4**

Total cooking time **20 minutes**

2 tablespoons **vegetable oil**

2 **garlic cloves**, finely chopped

2 **shallots**, thinly sliced

1 **carrot**, peeled and cut into thin matchsticks

3 inch length of trimmed **lemon grass stalk**, finely chopped

1 **red chile**, seeded and chopped

1 tablespoon **hot curry powder**

1 ¼ cups **coconut milk**

¾ cup **water**

1 tablespoon **fish sauce**

2 ¼ lb **raw jumbo shrimp**, peeled and deveined, with tails left on

1 cup cubed **mango** flesh (about 10 oz)

**Thai basil leaves**, to garnish

steamed **jasmine rice**, to serve

**Heat** the oil in a heavy saucepan, add the garlic, shallots, and carrot and cook over medium heat, stirring occasionally, for 1–2 minutes, until softened. Add the lemon grass, red chile, and curry powder and cook for another 3 minutes or until fragrant.

**Pour** in the coconut milk, measured water, and fish sauce and bring to a simmer. Cook for 5 minutes, then reduce the heat to medium-low, stir in the shrimp and mango and simmer gently, partially covered, for 5 minutes or until the shrimp turn pink and are cooked through.

**Ladle** into bowls, sprinkle with Thai basil leaves, and serve with steamed jasmine rice.

**For shrimp, lemon grass & mango stir-fry**, heat 2 tablespoons sunflower oil in a large wok until hot, add 2 chopped shallots, 2 seeded and chopped red chiles, 2 chopped garlic cloves, and a 3 inch length of trimmed lemon grass stalk, finely chopped, and stir-fry over high heat for 1 minute. Add 1 tablespoon hot curry powder, 1 lb 5 oz cooked peeled shrimp, and the diced flesh of 1 ripe mango and stir-fry for another 3–4 minutes or until piping hot. Serve with noodles. **Total cooking time 10 minutes.**

# cajun spiced salmon frittata

Serves **4**
Total cooking time **20 minutes**

1 tablespoon **olive oil**
1 **red bell pepper**, cored,
    seeded, and cut into chunks
1 **green bell pepper**, cored,
    seeded, and cut into chunks
1 small **onion**, sliced
1 small **red chile**, seeded and
    finely chopped
6 tablespoons chopped **fresh
    cilantro**, plus extra to garnish
8 oz **skinless salmon fillets**
1 inch piece of **fresh ginger
    root**, peeled and coarsely
    chopped
2 teaspoons **Cajun spice mix**
6 **eggs**
**pepper**
**salad**, to serve (optional)

**Heat** the oil in a 9 inch nonstick skillet and cook the peppers, onion, and chile over medium heat, stirring occasionally, for 3–4 minutes, until beginning to soften. Stir in the cilantro, then make a well in the center of the pan, add the salmon fillets and cook for 3–4 minutes, turning once, until almost cooked through.

**Flake** the fillets into chunky pieces in the pan, then add the ginger and spice mix and gently toss all the ingredients together.

**Beat** the eggs in a bowl and season with a little pepper. Pour over the vegetables and salmon and gently cook for 3–4 minutes, until the base of the frittata is set.

**Place** the pan under a preheated medium broiler, making sure that the pan handle is turned away from the heat, and cook for 4–5 minutes, until the top is golden and set. Cut into wedges and serve with salad, if desired.

**For simple Cajun salmon**, mix a squeeze of ginger paste with 2 teaspoons Cajun spice mix and rub into the flesh of 8 oz skinless salmon fillets. Heat 3 tablespoons olive oil in a large skillet and cook the salmon over medium heat for 9 minutes, turning halfway through. Serve with bread and salad. **Total cooking time 10 minutes.**

# roasted garlicky herb sea bass

Serves **2**

Total cooking time **30 minutes**

2 **whole sea bass**, about
   10 oz each, gutted
1 **garlic clove**, sliced
¼ cup chopped **parsley**
2 tablespoons chopped
   **thyme leaves**
1 **lemon**, halved and sliced
1 **fennel bulb**, trimmed and
   thinly sliced
12 oz **potatoes**, cut into slim
   wedges
1 tablespoon **olive oil**
**salt** and **pepper**

**Place** the fish in a roasting pan and slash both sides deep to the bone. Season well with pepper.

**Mix** together the garlic and herbs in a bowl, then rub the mixture over the fish, pushing it into the slashes. Tuck the lemon slices and fennel under and around the fish.

**Toss** the potatoes with the oil and season well, then arrange on top of the lemon and fennel.

**Roast** in a preheated oven, 400°F, for 20–25 minutes or until the potatoes are golden and the fish is cooked through.

**For pan-fried sea bass & fennel**, slash 2 gutted sea bass, about 10 oz each, several times on each side and season well. Heat 2 tablespoons butter in a large skillet, add 1 small trimmed and thinly sliced fennel bulb and 1 thinly sliced garlic clove, and cook over medium heat for 3–4 minutes, until slightly softened. Add the fish to the pan and cook for 4 minutes on each side or until the flesh is opaque and cooked through. Sprinkle with 1 tablespoon chopped thyme leaves and season well. Serve with crusty bread. **Total cooking time 20 minutes.**

# thai green curry with angler fish

Serves **4**

Total cooking time **30 minutes**

2 tablespoons **Thai green curry paste**

handful of chopped **fresh cilantro**

1 tablespoon **vegetable oil**

1¼ cups **fish** or **chicken stock**

1⅔ cups **coconut milk**

2 tablespoons **fish sauce**

2 teaspoons **brown sugar**

1 lb **skinless angler fish fillet**, cut into 1 inch cubes

3 oz **cherry tomatoes**, halved

handful of chopped **basil**, to garnish

**Put** the Thai green curry paste and cilantro in a mini food processor and blend to a smooth paste.

**Heat** the oil in a large saucepan. Add the curry paste and stir around the pan for 3–5 minutes, until the oil starts to separate. Pour over the stock and coconut milk and bring to a boil. Add the fish sauce and sugar and let simmer for 10 minutes.

**Stir** in the fish and tomatoes and cook for another 7–10 minutes, until just cooked through. Sprinkle with the basil and serve.

**For angler fish & bean curry**, heat 2 tablespoons vegetable oil in a large saucepan. Add 2 tablespoons Thai green curry paste and cook for 3 minutes, until the oil starts to separate. Pour over 1¼ cups fish or chicken stock, 1⅔ cups coconut milk, 2 tablespoons fish sauce, and 2 teaspoons brown sugar. Simmer for 10 minutes. Add 1¼ cups green beans and cook for 1–2 minutes. Stir in 1 lb skinless angler fish fillet, cut into 1 inch cubes, and cook for 3–5 minutes. Sprinkle with a handful of basil leaves to serve. **Total cooking time 20 minutes.**

# chili cod in tomato sauce

Serves **4**

Total cooking time **30 minutes**

2 tablespoons **olive oil**

1 **onion**, diced

2 **garlic cloves**, crushed

¼ teaspoon **dried red pepper flakes**

1 **red bell pepper**, cored, seeded, and thinly sliced

1 (14½ oz) can **diced tomatoes**

6 tablespoons **white wine**

12 **black ripe olives**, pitted and sliced

4 **skinless cod loin fillets**, about 5 oz each

steamed **green beans**, to serve (optional)

**Heat** the olive oil in a large skillet and sauté the onion, garlic, and red pepper flakes for 3–4 minutes. Add the bell pepper and cook for another 3–4 minutes.

**Pour** in the diced tomatoes, white wine, and black olives and simmer for 8 minutes.

**Add** the cod loin fillets to the pan and cook for 8–10 minutes, turning once if not covered by the liquid, until cooked through. Serve with steamed green beans, if desired.

**For pesto-crusted cod,** heat 1 tablespoon olive oil in a flameproof skillet and cook 4 (5 oz) cod fillets for 2–3 minutes. Mix together ¼ cup fresh bread crumbs with ½ red chile, seeded and finely diced, 2 tablespoons ready-made pesto, and 3 sliced scallions. Spoon the bread-crumb mixture over the fish and press down lightly. Sprinkle with 1 tablespoon grated Parmesan cheese and cook under a preheated hot broiler for 2–3 minutes, until golden and cooked through. Serve with a crisp green salad. **Total cooking time 10 minutes.**

# scallop, bacon & pine nut pan-fry

Serves **4**
Total cooking time **10 minutes**

2 tablespoons **butter**
10 oz **smoked bacon**, cut
  into pieces
12 oz **scallops**, halved
  widthwise if large
¼ cup **pine nuts**
½ cup chopped **parsley**
finely grated zest of **1 lemon**
**crusty bread**, to serve

**Heat** the butter in a large skillet, add the bacon and cook over high heat for 3 minutes, until golden.

**Add** the scallops and pine nuts and cook for 3–4 minutes, until the scallops are cooked through and the pine nuts are golden. Stir in the parsley and lemon zest. Divide the mixture among 4 dishes, spoon over any juices and serve with plenty of crusty bread.

**For grilled scallops in bacon**, place 16 large scallops, 2 tablespoons chopped parsley, and the finely grated zest of 1 lemon in a bowl and toss well to coat. Wrap 1 bacon slice around each scallop, then secure with toothpicks. Heat 2 tablespoons butter in a ridged grill pan, add the scallops and cook over high heat for 2 minutes on each side, until golden and cooked through. Serve with salad and crusty bread. **Total cooking time 20 minutes.**

# cod, red snapper & shrimp stew

Serves **4**

Total cooking time **20 minutes**

1 tablespoon **olive oil**

1 **fennel bulb**, quartered and
thinly sliced

2 **garlic cloves**, thinly sliced

1 (14½ oz) can **diced
tomatoes**

pinch of **saffron threads**

3¾ cups hot **fish stock**

8 oz **cod loin**, cut into
bite-size pieces

7 oz **cooked peeled jumbo
shrimp**

2 **red snapper fillets**, halved
lengthwise

1 cup **spinach leaves**

**crusty whole-wheat bread**,
to serve

**Heat** the oil in a large skillet, add the fennel and garlic
and cook for 4–5 minutes, until softened. Stir in the
tomatoes and saffron, then pour in the stock and bring
to a simmer.

**Add** the cod, shrimp, and red snapper and simmer for
6–8 minutes or until the fish is cooked through.

**Stir** in the spinach until wilted, then serve immediately
with crusty whole-wheat bread.

### For quick cod, red snapper & shrimp curry, heat
1 tablespoon oil in a large skillet or wok, add 1 chopped
onion and 2 chopped garlic cloves and sauté for 1 minute.
Stir in 2 tablespoons curry paste and 1⅔ cups coconut
milk and bring to a simmer. Add 7 oz cod loin and 2 red
snapper fillets, each cut into bite-size pieces, and 8 oz
cooked peeled jumbo shrimp. Simmer for 6–8 minutes,
until the fish is cooked through. Stir in 2½ cups spinach
leaves and 2 tablespoons coarsely chopped cilantro.
Season and serve with rice. **Total cooking time
10 minutes.**

# quick fish stew with chickpeas

Serves **4**

Total cooking time **20 minutes**

2 tablespoons **olive oil**

1 **celery stick**, thinly sliced

2 **garlic cloves**, chopped

1 teaspoon **sweet paprika**

½ cup **dry white wine**

1 (13 oz) can **good-quality ratatouille** or **plum tomatoes with herbs**

1 (15 oz) can **chickpeas**, rinsed and drained

1 teaspoon grated **lemon** zest

5 tablespoons **vegetable stock**

13 oz **boneless fish fillets**, such as haddock, cod, or salmon, cut into bite-size pieces

**salt** and **pepper**

chopped **parsley**, to garnish

**whole-grain rice** or **couscous**, to serve

**Heat** the oil in a large saucepan and cook the celery and garlic over medium heat for 3–4 minutes, to soften.

**Add** the paprika, stir for 1 minute, then pour in the wine and simmer to reduce by half.

**Tip** in the ratatouille along with the chickpeas, lemon zest, and stock, then season with salt and pepper to taste and simmer for 5–6 minutes, to thicken slightly.

**Stir** the fish into the stew, cover, and simmer for another 3–5 minutes or until the fish is cooked and flaky. Garnish with chopped parsley and serve with rice or couscous.

**For baked fish with chickpeas**, prepare the stew following the recipe above, adding 1 small diced head of fennel to the celery and garlic and cooking for 5–6 minutes before adding the paprika. Once the stew has simmered for 5–6 minutes, transfer it to an ovenproof dish and place 4 skinless, boneless fish fillets on top. Drizzle with 1 tablespoon olive oil, season and bake, uncovered, in a preheated oven, 400°F, for 12–15 minutes. Serve with rice or couscous and garnished with chopped parsley. **Total cooking time 30 minutes.**

# spicy shrimp & pea pilau

Serves **4**
Total cooking time **30 minutes**

1 tablespoon **sunflower oil**
1 tablespoon **butter**
1 **large onion**, finely chopped
2 **garlic cloves**, finely chopped
1 tablespoon **medium** or **hot curry paste**
1¼ cups **basmati rice**
2½ cups hot **fish** or **vegetable stock**
2 cups **frozen peas**
finely grated zest and juice of 1 large **lime**
⅔ cup **fresh cilantro**, finely chopped
13 oz **cooked peeled shrimp**
**salt** and **pepper**

**Heat** the oil and butter in a heavy saucepan, add the onion and cook over medium heat for 2–3 minutes, until softened. Stir in the garlic and curry paste and cook for another 1–2 minutes until fragrant, then add the rice and stir to coat well.

**Stir** in the stock, peas, and lime zest, then season well and bring to a boil. Cover tightly, then reduce the heat to low and cook for 12–15 minutes or until the liquid is absorbed and the rice is tender.

**Remove** the pan from the heat, then stir in the lime juice, cilantro, and shrimp. Cover and leave the shrimp to heat through for a few minutes before serving.

**For spicy shrimp & pea stir-fried rice**, heat 2 tablespoons sunflower oil in a large wok or skillet until hot, add 1 tablespoon medium curry paste, 12 oz cooked peeled shrimp, 1⅓ cups frozen peas, and 3¾ cups ready-cooked basmati rice and stir-fry over high heat for 4–5 minutes or until piping hot. Remove from the heat, season and stir in 6 tablespoons chopped fresh cilantro. Serve immediately. **Total cooking time 10 minutes.**

# vegetarian

# spiced coconut squash soup

Serves **4–6**

Total cooking time **20 minutes**

2 tablespoons **oil**

1 **onion**, chopped

2 teaspoons finely chopped
   **fresh ginger root**

½ teaspoon **ground coriander**

1 **lemon grass stalk**

1 strip of **orange** peel

2 lb **butternut squash**, peeled
   and chopped

4 cups **vegetable stock**

½ cup **coconut milk**

**salt** and **pepper**

**To serve**

1 **red chile**, seeded and
   chopped

handful of chopped **fresh
   cilantro**

**Heat** the oil in a large saucepan, add the onion and cook for 5 minutes, until softened. Add the ginger, ground coriander, lemon grass, orange peel, and squash. Pour in the stock and coconut milk and bring to a boil. Let simmer for 12–15 minutes, until the squash is soft.

**Remove** the lemon grass and orange peel and use an immersion blender to blend the soup until smooth. Season to taste and divide among serving bowls. Sprinkle with the chile and fresh cilantro to serve.

**For coconut squash rice pot**, heat 2 tablespoons oil in a large saucepan, add 1 chopped onion and cook for 5 minutes until softened. Stir in 1 crushed garlic clove and 1 teaspoon finely chopped fresh ginger root, followed by 2 tablespoons Thai red curry paste. Add ½ peeled and chopped butternut squash and cook for a couple of minutes until well coated. Stir through 1½ cups jasmine rice. Pour over 2 cups vegetable stock and ½ cup coconut milk. Bring to a boil and cook for 10 minutes, then reduce the heat and simmer gently for 5 minutes, until the rice and squash are just cooked through. Sprinkle with a handful of chopped fresh cilantro leaves before serving. **Total cooking time 30 minutes.**

# k garlicky tomato lentils

Serves **4**

Total cooking time **10 minutes**

2 tablespoons **olive** or
  **vegetable oil**

1 large **onion**, chopped

2 **garlic cloves**, chopped

2 cups **tomato-based
  pasta sauce**

1 teaspoon **dried oregano** or
  **mixed herbs** (optional)

2 (14½ oz) cans **green lentils**,
  rinsed and drained

1 cup grated **cheddar
  cheese, Parmesan cheese**,
  or **other hard Italian cheese**
  (optional)

**crusty bread**, to serve

**Heat** the oil in a large skillet and cook the onion and garlic over medium heat for 6–7 minutes, stirring frequently, until softened. Add the pasta sauce, dried oregano or mixed herbs, if using, and lentils and heat to simmering point.

**Spoon** into bowls. Sprinkle with grated cheese, if using, and serve immediately with crusty bread.

**For garlicky tomato rice**, heat 2 tablespoons olive or vegetable oil in a large saucepan and cook 1 large chopped onion and 1 cored, seeded, and chopped red, green, or yellow bell pepper for 6–7 minutes, until they begin to soften. Add 2 chopped garlic cloves and cook for another minute, then stir in 1¼ cups long-grain white rice. Add 2 (14½ oz) cans diced tomatoes, 1 teaspoon dried oregano or mixed herbs, 1¾ cups boiling water, and 1 crumbled vegetable bouillon cube. Stir well to combine, then reduce the heat, cover with a lid and simmer gently for 18–20 minutes, until the rice is tender and most of the liquid has been absorbed. Spoon into bowls and serve with a hot chili sauce. **Total cooking time 30 minutes.**

# spinach & potato tortilla

Serves **4**
Total cooking time **20 minutes**

3 tablespoons **olive oil**
2 **onions**, finely chopped
8 oz **cooked potatoes**, peeled
   and cut into ½ inch cubes
2 **garlic cloves**, finely chopped
½ cup **cooked spinach**,
   drained thoroughly and
   coarsely chopped
¼ cup drained and finely
   chopped **roasted red**
   **pepper**, from a jar
5 **eggs**, lightly beaten
3–4 tablespoons grated
   **Manchego cheese**
**salt** and **pepper**

**Heat** the oil in a nonstick skillet and add the onions and potatoes. Cook gently over medium heat for 3–4 minutes or until the vegetables have softened but not colored, turning and stirring often.

**Add** the garlic, spinach, and peppers and stir to mix well.

**Season** the beaten eggs and pour into the skillet, shaking the pan so that the egg is evenly spread. Cook gently for 8–10 minutes or until the base of the tortilla is set.

**Sprinkle** over the grated Manchego. Place the pan under a preheated medium-hot broiler and cook for 3–4 minutes or until the top is set and golden.

**Remove** from the heat, cut into bite-size squares or triangles and serve warm or at room temperature.

**For spinach & potato sauté**, heat 1 tablespoon vegetable oil in a large skillet. Add 2 chopped garlic cloves, 1 finely chopped onion, and 1 tablespoon curry powder. Stir in 6 tablespoons tomato puree or tomato sauce, 6 cups baby leaf spinach, and 7 oz cooked, cubed potatoes. Sauté over high heat for 2–3 minutes or until piping hot. Season and serve with crusty bread or rice. **Total cooking time 10 minutes.**

# coconut soup with squash

Serves **4**

Total cooking time **20 minutes**

1 tablespoon **vegetable oil**
1 **onion**, finely chopped
1 lb **butternut squash**,
  peeled, seeded, and cut
  into cubes
1 small **red chile**, seeded
  and finely chopped
1 teaspoon **ground coriander**
1⅔ cups **coconut milk**
2½ cups **vegetable stock**
6 cups **spinach leaves**
warm **naan breads**, to serve

**Heat** the oil in a large, heavy saucepan and cook the onion, butternut squash, and chile over medium-high heat, stirring frequently, for 8 minutes, until softened. Add the coriander and cook, stirring, for a few seconds, then stir in the coconut milk and stock and bring to a boil. Reduce the heat and simmer for 10 minutes.

**Stir** in the spinach leaves and cook for 1 minute, until just wilted. Ladle the soup into serving bowls and serve with warm naan breads.

**For quick Caribbean-style coconut soup**, heat 1 tablespoon vegetable oil in a large, heavy saucepan and cook 1 finely chopped red onion over medium-high heat, stirring frequently, for 3 minutes. Add 1 teaspoon ground coriander and ½ teaspoon smoked paprika and cook, stirring, for a few seconds. Stir in 1⅔ cups coconut milk and 2½ cups vegetable stock and bring to a boil. Add 1 (15 oz) can kidney beans, rinsed and drained, with 6 cups spinach leaves and simmer for 5 minutes. Serve with corn bread. **Total cooking time 10 minutes.**

# quick pea & leek soup

Serves **4**

Total cooking time **10 minutes**

3½ tablespoons **butter**

2 **banana shallots**, finely chopped

2 **leeks**, very thinly sliced

1 tablespoon chopped **mixed herbs**, such as sage, thyme, chives, and parsley

6 tablespoons **sour cream**

4 cups good-quality boiling **vegetable stock**

2½ cups **frozen petits pois**

**salt** and **pepper**

**Melt** the butter in a large saucepan over medium heat, then add the shallots and leeks and cook for 5–6 minutes, until softened.

**Meanwhile,** stir the chopped herbs into the sour cream and set aside.

**Add** the vegetable stock and petits pois to the leeks and simmer for 2–3 minutes, until the peas are just tender.

**Season** to taste, then ladle into bowls and serve immediately with a dollop of herby sour cream.

**For potato, pea & leek soup**, heat 2 tablespoons olive oil in a large saucepan or flameproof casserole dish and add 1¾ lb diced potatoes, 2 chopped leeks, and 3 thinly sliced scallions. Cook over medium heat for 5 minutes, stirring frequently, until the leek is beginning to soften. Add 5 cups boiling vegetable stock, season, and simmer over medium heat for about 12 minutes, until the potato is tender, adding 1 cup frozen peas for the final 2–3 minutes. Blend the soup until smooth, then ladle into bowls and serve with herby sour cream, as above. **Total cooking time 20 minutes.**

# quick carrot & coriander tagine

Serves **4**

Total cooking time **20 minutes**

2 tablespoons **olive oil**

1¾ lb **carrots**, peeled and
  sliced

1 inch piece of **fresh ginger
  root**, peeled and finely
  chopped

2 **garlic cloves**, sliced

2 teaspoons **baharat** or **ras
  el hanout**

1 teaspoon **ground coriander**

pinch of **saffron threads**
  (optional)

8 **ready-to-eat dried apricots**,
  sliced

1 **preserved lemon**, chopped

1⅔ cups hot **vegetable stock**

handful of chopped **fresh
  cilantro**, to garnish

steamed **giant couscous**,
  to serve

**Heat** the oil in a large saucepan or flameproof
casserole dish and cook the carrots, ginger, and garlic
for 5–6 minutes, until beginning to soften. Add the
spices and apricots and stir for a minute before adding
the preserved lemon and hot stock. Cover and simmer
for 10–12 minutes, until tender.

**Ladle** the tagine into bowls, sprinkle with the cilantro,
and serve with giant couscous.

**For Moroccan-style carrot & coriander soup**, heat
2 tablespoons olive oil in a large saucepan or flameproof
casserole dish and add 1 chopped onion, 1 tablespoon
peeled and chopped fresh ginger root, and 2 chopped
garlic cloves. Cook over medium heat for 7–8 minutes,
until softened. Stir in 1 teaspoon ras el hanout and
1 teaspoon ground coriander, then add 1½ lb peeled
and chopped carrots and 1 peeled and chopped sweet
potato. Stir to coat, then pour in 5 cups hot vegetable
stock. Cover and simmer over medium heat for about
15 minutes, until the vegetables are tender. Blend the
soup with an immersion blender, then season to taste
and ladle into bowls. Garnish with plenty of chopped
fresh cilantro to serve. **Total cooking time 30 minutes.**

# pan-cooked eggs

Serves **2**
Total cooking time **10 minutes**

2 tablespoons **butter**
1 **leek**, thinly sliced
¼ teaspoon **dried red
pepper flakes**
6 cups **baby spinach leaves**
2 **eggs**
3 tablespoons **plain yogurt**
pinch of **ground paprika**
**salt** and **pepper**

**Heat** the butter in a skillet, add the leek and red pepper flakes, and cook over medium-high heat for 4–5 minutes, until softened. Add the spinach and season well with salt and pepper, then toss and cook for 2 minutes, until wilted.

**Make** 2 wells in the vegetables and break an egg into each well. Cook over low heat for 2–3 minutes, until the eggs are set. Spoon the yogurt on top and sprinkle with the paprika.

**For leek & spinach omelet**, heat 1 tablespoon olive oil in a large skillet, add 1 small leek, very thinly sliced, and cook over medium heat for 3–4 minutes, then add 3½ cups baby spinach leaves and cook for 2 minutes, stirring, until wilted. In a bowl, beat together 4 eggs and season well, then pour over the spinach mixture. Cook over low heat for 2–3 minutes, until the base is set, then place a baking sheet over the top of the pan and cook for another 1 minute until the top is set. Gently flip one side of the omelet over onto the other, then cut the omelet in half. Lightly toast 2 pieces of walnut bread and spread each with 1 tablespoon tomato chutney, then place an omelet half over each. **Total cooking time 20 minutes.**

# red pepper & spinach stew

Serves **4**
Total cooking time **20 minutes**

3 tablespoons **olive** or
   **vegetable oil**
2 large **red bell peppers**,
   cored, seeded, and cut into
   large pieces
3 **garlic cloves**, sliced
2 teaspoons **ground cumin** or
   **Mexican spice mix**, such as
   fajita seasoning (optional)
2 tablespoons **tomato paste**
2⅔ cups **vegetable stock**
1 (14½ oz) can **diced
   tomatoes**
2½ cups **canned kidney
   beans**, rinsed and drained
¾ cup **frozen leaf spinach**,
   defrosted and drained
**salt** and **pepper**

**Heat** the oil in a saucepan and cook the peppers and garlic over medium heat for 5–6 minutes, stirring frequently, until softened.

**Stir** in the cumin, if using, and cook for 1 minute before adding the tomato paste, hot stock, diced tomatoes, and kidney beans. Bring to a boil, season to taste, then cover and simmer gently for 10–12 minutes, until thickened slightly. Stir in the spinach for the final minute of cooking, then ladle into bowls to serve.

**For red pepper & kidney bean soup**, cook the peppers and garlic as above until softened. Add the ground cumin and cook for a minute, then pour in 3 cups hot vegetable stock, 2 cups sieved tomatoes or tomato sauce, and 2 (15 oz) cans kidney beans, rinsed and drained, reserving about ¾ cup of the beans. Season to taste, then cover, bring to a boil and simmer for about 15 minutes, until slightly thickened. Use an immersion blender to blend the soup, then stir through the reserved beans, ½ cup defrosted chopped spinach and heat through. Ladle into bowls to serve, sprinkled with chopped parsley. **Total cooking time 30 minutes.**

# quick mushroom & garlic tom yum

Serves **4**
Total cooking time **10 minutes**

1 tablespoon **tom yum paste**
4 cups **vegetable stock**
5 oz **oyster mushrooms**, sliced
7 oz **closed-cup mushrooms**, sliced
3½ oz **enoki mushrooms** (optional)
2 **scallions**, thinly sliced
2 **garlic cloves**, sliced
1 inch piece **fresh ginger root**, peeled and sliced
**lime juice**, to serve

**Place** the tom yum paste in a large saucepan with the stock and bring to a simmer. Add the mushrooms, scallions, garlic, and ginger and simmer for 5–6 minutes, so the flavors develop and the mushrooms soften.

**Ladle** into bowls and serve immediately with a squeeze of lime juice.

**For wild mushroom & garlic broth**, place ⅔ cup mixed dried mushrooms in a pan with 4 cups just simmering water. Cover and cook for 10 minutes, until softened. Meanwhile, heat 2 tablespoons oil in a saucepan and cook 1 diced celery stick, 1 sliced leek, 2 chopped shallots, and 2 chopped garlic cloves for 7–8 minutes over medium heat until softened. Add 10 oz sliced portobello mushrooms and cook for another 2 minutes, until just beginning to soften. Strain the dried mushrooms, reserving the liquid, then slice and add to the vegetables. Stir, then add the reserved mushroom stock and simmer for 4–5 minutes. Ladle into bowls and serve. **Total cooking time 20 minutes.**

# red cabbage & beet lentils

Serves **2**
Total cooking time **20 minutes**

2 tablespoons **olive** or
**vegetable oil**
½ small **red cabbage**, thinly
sliced
2 **scallions**, sliced, plus extra
to garnish
1 **beet**, coarsely shredded
1 teaspoon **ground cumin**
1½ cups **canned green
lentils**, rinsed and drained
**salt** and **pepper**
**plain** or **Greek yogurt**, to
serve

**Heat** the oil in a saucepan and cook the red cabbage
and scallion over medium heat for about 5 minutes, until
just beginning to soften. Stir in the beet, then cover and
cook for another 8–10 minutes, stirring occasionally,
until the vegetables are tender.

**Sprinkle** with the ground cumin and stir over the heat
for a minute, then add the lentils and warm through.
Season to taste, then spoon into 2 dishes and serve
with a dollop of yogurt and extra sliced scallions.

**For fruity braised red cabbage,** heat 2 tablespoons
olive or vegetable oil in a saucepan and gently cook
1 finely chopped red onion over medium heat for
6–7 minutes, until softened. Add 1 chopped garlic
clove and 1 teaspoon ground cumin, then stir in
½ shredded red cabbage, 1 peeled and coarsely
shredded dessert apple, and a small handful of raisins.
Cook gently for about 15 minutes, stirring frequently,
until the vegetables are softened but still have some
bite. Season to taste, then stir in 2 teaspoons balsamic
vinegar and serve with broiled vegetarian sausages.
**Total cooking time 30 minutes.**

# black-eyed pea stew

Serves **4**

Total cooking time **30 minutes**

2 tablespoons **olive oil**

4 **shallots**, finely chopped

2 **garlic cloves**, crushed

2 **celery sticks**, diced

1 large **carrot**, peeled and cut into ½ inch pieces

1 **red bell pepper**, cored, seeded, and cut into ½ inch pieces

1 teaspoon **dried mixed herbs**

2 teaspoons **ground cumin**

1 teaspoon **ground cinnamon**

2 (14½ oz) cans **tomatoes**

2 tablespoons **tomato paste**

5 tablespoons **vegetable stock**

2 (15 oz) cans **black-eyed peas in water**, rinsed and drained

¼ cup finely chopped **fresh cilantro**, plus extra leaves to garnish

**salt** and **pepper**

**basmati rice**, to serve

**Heat** the oil in a large skillet and place over high heat.

**Add** the shallots, garlic, celery, carrot, and bell pepper and stir-fry for 2–3 minutes or until lightly starting to brown.

**Sprinkle** in the dried herbs, cumin, and cinnamon, add the tomatoes, tomato paste, and stock and bring to a boil. Reduce the heat to medium, cover, and cook gently for 12–15 minutes or until the vegetables are tender, breaking up the tomatoes into small pieces with a wooden spoon toward the end of the cooking time.

**Stir** in the black-eyed peas and cook for 2–3 minutes or until piping hot.

**Season** well with salt and pepper, remove from the heat, and sprinkle with the chopped cilantro. Garnish with cilantro leaves and serve with basmati rice.

**For hearty bean & vegetable broth**, place 1 peeled and finely diced carrot, 2 finely diced celery sticks, 2 finely diced shallots, 2 crushed garlic cloves, 2 tablespoons tomato paste, and 2 teaspoons dried mixed herbs in a heavy saucepan with 4 cups hot vegetable stock and bring to a boil. Cook, uncovered, over medium heat for 10–12 minutes. Stir in 2 (15 oz) cans black-eyed peas, rinsed and drained, and bring back to a boil. Season, remove from the heat and serve ladled into bowls with crusty bread. **Total cooking time 20 minutes.**

# savoy cabbage & parmesan soup

Serves **4**

Total cooking time **30 minutes**

¼ cup **olive oil**

1 **onion**, chopped

2 **garlic cloves**, crushed

½ teaspoon **fennel seeds**

1 **Savoy cabbage**

1 **potato**, peeled and diced

4 cups **vegetable stock**

¾ cup grated **Parmesan cheese**, plus extra 1 tablespoon to serve

**salt** and **pepper**

**crusty bread**, to serve

**Heat** 2 tablespoons of the olive oil in a saucepan and sauté the onion, garlic, and fennel seeds for 3–4 minutes.

**Shred** 4 leaves of the cabbage and reserve. Finely shred the remaining cabbage, add to the pan with the diced potato and cook for 3–4 minutes, then pour in the stock.

**Simmer** for 10 minutes, until the potato is tender. Stir in the grated Parmesan.

**Blend** with an immersion blender, or in a food processor, until smooth. Season with salt and pepper to taste.

**Heat** the remaining olive oil and stir-fry the reserved cabbage. Top each bowl of soup with the fried cabbage.

**Serve** sprinkled with extra grated Parmesan, and slices of crusty bread on the side.

**For rice with Savoy cabbage**, heat 3 tablespoons olive oil in a skillet and sauté 1 chopped onion for 2–3 minutes. Stir in 4 cups finely shredded Savoy cabbage and cook, stirring, until wilted. Stir in 1¼ cups Arborio rice and 4 cups vegetable stock. Bring to a boil and simmer for 15–16 minutes, until the rice is al dente. Stir in 2 tablespoons butter and ½ cup grated Parmesan, season and serve. **Total cooking time 20 minutes.**

# bean & vegetable nut crumble

Serves **4**
Total cooking time **30 minutes**

5 tablespoons **butter**, chilled
   and diced
1⅓ cups **all-purpose flour**
1 cup **walnuts**, chopped
½ cup shredded **cheddar
   cheese**
1 lb **prepared broccoli,
   cauliflower, and carrots**
2 cups **ready-made tomato
   and herb sauce**
2 **garlic cloves**, crushed
6 tablespoons finely chopped
   **basil leaves**
1 (15 oz) can **lima beans**,
   rinsed and drained
**salt** and **pepper**

**Blend** the butter into the flour until crumbs form.
Stir in the chopped walnuts and shredded cheese,
season, and set aside.

**Remove** the carrots from the prepared vegetables,
coarsely chop, and boil in a large saucepan for
2 minutes. Add the broccoli and cauliflower and cook
for another minute, then drain.

**Pour** the tomato and herb sauce over the blanched
vegetables and heat until bubbling.

**Stir** in the garlic, basil, and lima beans. Transfer to
a medium-size ovenproof dish and sprinkle with the
crumble mixture. Bake in a preheated oven, 400°F,
for 15–20 minutes or until golden and bubbling.

**For lima bean & walnut pâté**, put 2 (15 oz) cans lima
beans, rinsed and drained, and the juice and finely grated
zest of 1 lemon into a food processor with 1 crushed
garlic clove, ¼ cup each of finely chopped basil and
mint leaves, ⅓ cup chopped walnuts, ½ cup ready-made
mayonnaise, and 2 teaspoons Dijon mustard. Blend
until fairly smooth and serve spread thickly on toasted
sourdough bread with a salad. **Total cooking time
10 minutes.**

# malaysian stew

Serves **4**

Total cooking time **30 minutes**

2 tablespoons **vegetable oil**

1 **medium onion**, thinly sliced

6 tablespoons **laksa curry paste**

3⅓ cups **coconut milk**

1¼ cups **water**

1 teaspoon **salt**

1 cup peeled, cubed **potatoes**

1 cup peeled, cubed **carrots**

1 cup **green beans**, topped, tailed, and halved

½ cup **cauliflower florets**

2 cups cubed **butternut squash**

⅓ cup **cashew nuts**

½ cup **bean sprouts**

4 **scallions**, trimmed and sliced on the diagonal

handful of **Thai sweet basil leaves** or **fresh cilantro**

**Heat** the oil in a large saucepan over medium heat. Add the onion and the curry paste and fry gently for 2–3 minutes, until it begins to smell fragrant.

**Pour** in the coconut milk and measured water, add the salt and bring to a boil.

**Add** the potatoes and carrots and cook for 10 minutes, then add the green beans, cauliflower, and squash and cook for another 7 minutes.

**Sprinkle** with the cashew nuts and simmer for 3 minutes, until the vegetables are just tender.

**Stir** in the bean sprouts, scallions, and basil or cilantro. Simmer for 1 minute and serve immediately.

**For quick Asian coconut soup**, heat 1 tablespoon vegetable oil in a large wok and add 6 chopped scallions, 1 tablespoon laksa curry paste, 1⅔ cups coconut milk, 1⅔ cups vegetable stock, and 10 oz pack stir-fry vegetables. Bring to a boil and cook over high heat for 4–5 minutes. Season and serve. **Total cooking time 10 minutes.**

# southern-style rice

Serves **4**

Total cooking time **30 minutes**

1½ tablespoons **vegetable oil**

1 large **onion**, chopped

2 **garlic cloves**, coarsely chopped

1 **celery stick**, chopped

1 **red** and 1 **yellow bell pepper**, cored, seeded, and chopped

1 **zucchini**, chopped

1 teaspoon each **dried thyme, dried oregano, hot smoked paprika**

¼ teaspoon **cayenne pepper**

1¼ cups **long-grain rice**, rinsed

2 tablespoons **tomato paste**

2 (14½ oz) cans **diced tomatoes**

1¾ cups **vegetable stock**

**salt** and **pepper**

2 tablespoons chopped **parsley**, to garnish

few dashes **Tabasco sauce**, to serve (optional)

**Heat** the oil in a large, heavy casserole over medium heat. Add the onion, garlic, celery, and red and yellow peppers and cook for 4–5 minutes, stirring frequently, then add the zucchini and cook for another 3–4 minutes.

**Add** the herbs, spices, and rice and stir-fry for 1 minute, coating the rice well in the other ingredients. Stir in the tomato paste, diced tomatoes, and vegetable stock and season. Bring to a boil and cover with a tight-fitting lid, then reduce the heat and let simmer gently for 15–18 minutes, until the rice is cooked and the mixture thickened.

**Serve** sprinkled with chopped parsley and a few dashes of Tabasco sauce, if desired.

**For Southern-style mixed vegetable & bean stir-fry**, chop 1 large onion, 1 celery stick, and 1 zucchini. Core, seed, and chop 1 red and 1 yellow bell pepper and finely chop 2 garlic cloves. Coarsely chop 2 tablespoons pickled red jalapeño peppers and set aside. Heat 1½ tablespoons vegetable oil in a large skillet or wok over medium heat, then add the raw vegetables and stir-fry for 10 minutes, until tender. Add 1 teaspoon each of dried thyme, dried oregano, and hot smoked paprika and ¼ teaspoon cayenne pepper and stir-fry for another minute. Stir in 2 cups ready-cooked plain, mushroom, or chile and bean rice, then add 1 (15 oz) can kidney beans, rinsed and drained. Continue to stir-fry until hot, then serve immediately in bowls, each topped with a dollop of sour cream and a sprinkling of chopped pickled red jalapeño peppers. **Total cooking time 20 minutes.**

# tomato, rosemary & bean stew

Serves **4**

Total cooking time **10 minutes**

3 tablespoons **olive oil**
1 large **red onion**, sliced
2 teaspoons **garlic paste**
2 tablespoons chopped
   **rosemary leaves**
2 (15 oz) cans **cannellini
   beans**, rinsed and drained
2 cups **tomato pasta sauce**
**whole-wheat crusty bread**,
   to serve

**Heat** the oil in a large, heavy skillet and cook the onion over medium heat, stirring occasionally, for 2 minutes. Add the garlic paste and rosemary and cook, stirring constantly, for 30 seconds.

**Add** the beans and tomato sauce and bring to a boil. Reduce the heat, cover, and simmer for 6–7 minutes, until piping hot.

**Serve** with fresh whole-wheat bread for mopping up the juices.

**For cannellini bean cassoulet**, heat 3 tablespoons olive oil in a large, heavy skillet and cook 1 small chopped onion, 2 peeled and diced carrots, and 1 tablespoon chopped rosemary leaves over medium heat, stirring occasionally, for 3–4 minutes, until softened. Add 2 (15 oz) cans cannellini beans, rinsed and drained, with 2½ cups vegetable stock and bring to a boil. Simmer briskly, uncovered, for 10 minutes, until piping hot, then place a third of the beans into a food processor and blend until smooth. Return the pureed beans to the pan, stir to combine, and heat through. Season with salt and pepper to taste, then serve with crusty bread. **Total cooking time 20 minutes.**

# spicy mushroom & cauliflower

Serves **4**

Total cooking time **30 minutes**

2 tablespoons **sunflower oil**

8 **scallions**, cut into 2 inch
lengths

2 teaspoons **grated garlic**

2 teaspoons **ground ginger**

2 tablespoons **hot curry
powder**

7 oz **baby button mushrooms**

1 cup **cauliflower florets**

2 **red bell peppers**, cored,
seeded, and cut into chunks

1 (14½ oz) can **diced
tomatoes**

½ (15 oz) can **chickpeas**,
rinsed and drained

**salt** and **pepper**

large handful of chopped **mint
leaves**, to garnish

warm **naan bread**, to serve

**Heat** the oil in a large skillet, add the scallions, and fry over medium heat for 1–2 minutes. Add the garlic, ground ginger, and curry powder and fry, stirring, for 20–30 seconds, until fragrant, then stir in the mushrooms, cauliflower, and bell peppers and fry for another 2–3 minutes.

**Stir** in the tomatoes and bring to a boil. Cover, then reduce the heat to medium and simmer, uncovered, for 10–15 minutes, stirring occasionally. Add the chickpeas, season with salt and pepper and bring back to a boil.

**Sprinkle** with chopped mint and serve with warm naan.

**For spicy mushroom, cauliflower & chickpea rice**, heat 2 tablespoons sunflower oil in a large wok or skillet until hot, add 1 chopped onion, 1 seeded and chopped red chile, 3½ oz button mushrooms, 1 tablespoon curry powder, ⅓ cup small cauliflower florets, ½ cup canned chickpeas, rinsed and drained, 1 teaspoon ginger paste, and 1 teaspoon garlic paste and stir-fry over high heat for 6–8 minutes. Add 3¾ cups ready-cooked basmati or long-grain rice and stir-fry for another 3–4 minutes or until piping hot. Season, then serve immediately. **Total cooking time 20 minutes.**

# spicy szechuan tofu

Serves **4**

Total cooking time **20 minutes**

¼ cup **vegetable oil**

6 **scallions**, finely sliced

2 **red chiles**, seeded, and
thinly sliced

1 inch piece of **fresh ginger
root**, finely chopped

4 **garlic cloves**, finely sliced

1 teaspoon crushed **Szechuan
peppercorns**

pinch of **salt**

8 oz **firm tofu**, cut into 1 inch
cubes

2 cups **snow peas**, halved

1 cup **baby corn**, halved
lengthwise

4 cups chopped **bok choy**

3 cups **bean sprouts**

2 tablespoons **light soy sauce**

2 tablespoons **Shaohsing
rice wine**

**sesame oil**, for drizzling

steamed **rice**, to serve

**Heat** 2 tablespoons of the oil in a wok or deep skillet
and add the scallions, chiles, ginger, garlic, peppercorns,
and a pinch of salt. Fry for 1 minute, add the tofu, and
stir-fry for another 2 minutes, then transfer to a plate.

**Add** the remaining oil to the wok or skillet and stir-fry
the snow peas, corn, bok choy, and bean sprouts for
a few minutes, until starting to wilt, then add the soy
sauce and rice wine.

**Return** the tofu mixture to the wok or skillet and toss
everything together.

**Drizzle** with sesame oil and serve with rice.

**For speedy Szechuan stir-fry**, cube 1 lb firm tofu and
broil under a preheated medium broiler for 2–3 minutes,
until golden brown. Meanwhile, heat 2 tablespoons
vegetable oil in a wok or deep skillet. Add 2 (10 oz)
packs stir-fry vegetables and stir-fry for 3–4 minutes.
Stir in ⅔ cup ready-made Szechuan stir-fry sauce and
stir-fry for another 1–2 minutes. Add the tofu to the pan,
toss to mix and serve. **Total cooking time 10 minutes.**

# puffed goat cheese omelet

Serves **4**

Total cooking time **20 minutes**

6 eggs

¼ cup grated **Parmesan cheese**

handful of chopped **basil**

1 tablespoon **olive oil**

3 **roasted red peppers**, from a jar, drained and sliced

4 oz **soft goat cheese**

**salt** and **pepper**

**Crack** 3 eggs into a bowl. Separate the remaining 3 eggs and add the yolks to the whole eggs. Stir in the Parmesan and some of the basil and season to taste.

**Whisk** the egg whites until soft peaks form, then carefully fold into the whole egg mixture, one-third at a time.

**Heat** the oil in an ovenproof skillet. Add the egg mixture and cook for 2 minutes, then sprinkle with the peppers and goat cheese.

**Place** the pan under a preheated hot broiler and cook for 5–7 minutes more until puffed and just set. Sprinkle with the remaining basil to serve.

**For pecorino & chili omelets**, heat 1 tablespoon butter in a small skillet. Pour in 1 lightly beaten egg and stir around the pan. Let cook for 30 seconds, until starting to set, then grate over 1 oz pecorino cheese and add a pinch of dried red pepper flakes. Cook until the omelet is set, then roll it up and keep warm. Make 3 more omelets in the same way. Serve with a green salad. **Total cooking time 10 minutes.**

# spiced carrot & green bean stew

Serves **4**

Total cooking time **30 minutes**

1 tablespoon **sunflower oil**

1 **onion**, sliced

1–2 **hot green chiles**, seeded and sliced

1 **garlic clove**, crushed

5–6 **fresh curry leaves**

1 tablespoon **medium curry powder**

¼ teaspoon **ground turmeric**

½ teaspoon **fenugreek seeds**

2 **carrots**, peeled and cut into thin matchsticks

3 cups **green beans**, trimmed and halved

1⅔ cups **coconut milk**

juice of 1 **lime**

**salt** and **pepper**

steamed **rice** or **crusty bread**, to serve (optional)

**Heat** the oil in a heavy saucepan, add the onion, chiles, garlic, and curry leaves and cook over medium heat, stirring occasionally, for 6–8 minutes, until the onion is softened and golden brown. Sprinkle with the curry powder, turmeric, and fenugreek seeds and season well with salt and pepper.

**Add** the carrots and beans and cook, stirring, for another 3–4 minutes. Reduce the heat to low, pour over the coconut milk, and simmer for 10–12 minutes or until the vegetables are tender.

**Remove** from the heat and stir in the lime juice. Ladle into bowls and serve with steamed rice or bread, if desired.

**For spicy carrot & green bean soup**, heat 1 tablespoon butter and 1 tablespoon sunflower oil in a heavy saucepan, add 1 finely chopped onion, 1 chopped garlic clove, 1 teaspoon peeled and grated fresh ginger root, and 1 tablespoon mild curry powder and fry, stirring, for 1–2 minutes. Stir in 3 peeled and finely chopped carrots, 2 cups finely chopped trimmed green beans, and 3⅓ cups hot vegetable stock and bring to a boil, then reduce the heat to medium and cook for 12–15 minutes or until the vegetables are tender. Remove from the heat and, using an immersion blender, process the soup until smooth. Season, then stir in ¾ cup light cream. Serve with crusty bread. **Total cooking time 20 minutes.**

# chunky vegetable red lentil dahl

Serves **4**

Total cooking time **30 minutes**

¼ cup **vegetable oil**

1 large **onion**, coarsely chopped

1 **eggplant**, trimmed and coarsely chopped

1 **red bell pepper**, cored, seeded, and cut into chunks

8 oz **okra**, trimmed and cut into 1 inch lengths

¾ cup **split red lentils**, rinsed

3 tablespoons **balti curry paste**

2½ cups **vegetable stock**

3 tablespoons chopped **mint**

¾ cup **plain yogurt**

5 tablespoons chopped **fresh cilantro**

**salt** and **pepper**

warm **naan breads**, to serve

**Heat** the oil in a large, heavy saucepan and cook the onion and eggplant over medium heat, stirring occasionally, for 5 minutes, until softened and cooked through.

**Add** the bell pepper and okra to the pan and cook, stirring frequently, for 3–4 minutes before adding the lentils and curry paste. Stir well to mix, then pour in the stock. Bring to a boil, then reduce the heat, cover, and simmer for 20 minutes, until the lentils are tender.

**Meanwhile,** stir the mint into the yogurt.

**Remove** the pan from the heat, stir in the cilantro, and season to taste. Serve with warm naan breads and the minted yogurt for drizzling.

**For quick red lentil, chunky vegetable & chili soup**, heat 2 tablespoons olive oil in a saucepan and cook 2 chopped onions, 1 seeded and finely chopped red chile, the finely grated zest of 1 lemon, and 1 teaspoon ground cumin over medium heat, stirring, for 2 minutes. Add 1 cup rinsed split red lentils, 7 oz frozen chunky mixed vegetables, and 3 cups hot vegetable stock. Simmer for 8 minutes, until the lentils are tender. Stir through shredded mint and serve with plain yogurt and pita breads. **Total cooking time 10 minutes.**

# cauliflower & potato curry

Serves **4**
Total cooking time **30 minutes**

3 tablespoons **vegetable oil**
1 large **onion**, coarsely
 chopped
1 **cauliflower**, trimmed and
 cut into florets
1 lb **potatoes**, peeled and
 cut into chunks
2 teaspoons **cumin seeds**
¼ cup **korma curry paste**
1⅔ cups **coconut milk**
1¼ cups **vegetable stock**
6 cups **spinach leaves**
¼ cup chopped **fresh cilantro**
**salt** and **pepper**
warm **naan breads**, to serve

**Heat** the oil in a large, heavy saucepan and cook the onion over medium heat, stirring occasionally, for 2–3 minutes, until beginning to soften, then add the cauliflower, potatoes, and cumin seeds. Cook for 4–5 minutes, stirring occasionally, until the potatoes are beginning to brown.

**Add** the curry paste and toss to coat the vegetables, then stir in the coconut milk and stock and bring to a boil. Reduce the heat, cover, and simmer, stirring occasionally, for 20 minutes, until the vegetables are tender, adding the spinach for the last 5 minutes of the cooking time.

**Season** generously and stir in the cilantro. Serve with warm naan breads.

**For cauliflower Thai green curry**, cook a 1 lb mixture of frozen cauliflower florets and green beans in a large saucepan of slightly salted boiling water according to the pack instructions. Drain and return to the pan. Add 1½ cups Thai green curry sauce and heat through, stirring gently. Serve with ready-cooked Thai jasmine rice. **Total cooking time 10 minutes.**

# malaysian red pepper & cabbage

Serves **4**
Total cooking time **20 minutes**

1 tablespoon **sunflower oil**
2 **garlic cloves**, crushed
2 teaspoons **medium curry powder**
1 **red bell pepper**, cored, seeded, and finely diced
½ **green cabbage**, finely shredded
3 **eggs**, lightly beaten
**salt** and **pepper**
**crusty bread**, to serve (optional)

**Heat** the oil in a large wok or skillet until hot, add the garlic, curry powder, and bell pepper and stir-fry over medium-high heat for 3–4 minutes, until softened.

**Increase** the heat to high, add the cabbage, season with salt and pepper, and stir-fry for 5 minutes or until the cabbage is cooked but still retains a bite.

**Stir** in the eggs and mix well with the vegetables, then continue stirring until the eggs are scrambled and just cooked through. Serve immediately with crusty bread, if desired.

**For spicy cabbage & red pepper stew**, heat 2 tablespoons sunflower oil in a large saucepan, add 2 finely sliced onions and cook over medium heat, stirring occasionally, for 6–8 minutes or until soft and translucent. Stir in 3 chopped garlic cloves, 1 seeded and sliced red chile, and 1 tablespoon mild curry paste, then pour over 1⅔ cups hot vegetable stock and 1⅔ cups coconut milk and bring to a boil. Stir in ½ green cabbage, shredded, and 3 cored, seeded, and thinly sliced red bell peppers and bring back to a boil, then reduce the heat to medium and cook for 12–15 minutes or until the vegetables are tender. Season well, then serve with rice or crusty bread. **Total cooking time 30 minutes.**

# mushroom & tofu stew

Serves **4**

Total cooking time **20 minutes**

1 tablespoon **olive oil**

1 **onion**, sliced

500 g (1 lb) **brown mushrooms**, quartered

2¼ cups cubed **sweet potatoes**

½ tablespoon **pomegranate molasses** or **balsamic syrup**

1 tablespoon **whole-wheat flour**

2 cups hot **vegetable stock**

1 tablespoon **packed dark brown sugar**

dash of **Worcestershire sauce**

7 oz **tofu**, cubed

steamed **broccolini**, to serve

**Heat** the oil in a large saucepan or flameproof casserole dish, add the onion and cook for 1–2 minutes, until it starts to soften. Add the mushrooms and cook for another 1–2 minutes, stirring occasionally.

**Add** the sweet potatoes, molasses or syrup, and flour and stir well. Slowly pour in the stock, stirring continuously. Add the sugar and Worcestershire sauce and stir again until well mixed.

**Bring** to a simmer, cover, and cook for 15 minutes, until the sweet potatoes are tender. Add the tofu 5 minutes before the end of the cooking time.

**Serve** with steamed broccolini.

**For mushroom & tofu stir-fry**, heat 1 tablespoon coconut oil in a wok or large skillet, add 2 sliced red onions, 1 tablespoon mustard seeds, and 2 chopped garlic cloves and stir-fry for 1–2 minutes. Add 1 lb sliced brown mushrooms and stir-fry for 2–3 minutes, then add 1 cored, seeded, and sliced red bell pepper, ½ shredded Chinese cabbage, and 5 oz cubed tofu and stir-fry for another 4–5 minutes. Stir in 2 teaspoons soy sauce. Serve sprinkled with 2 tablespoons toasted sesame seeds. **Total cooking time 10 minutes.**

# jamaican spiced corn chowder

Serves **4**

Total cooking time **30 minutes**

1 tablespoon **olive oil**
1 large **onion**, finely chopped
2 **garlic cloves**, finely chopped
1 teaspoon **cayenne pepper**
1 cup **red split lentils**, rinsed
4 cups hot **vegetable stock**
1⅔ cups **coconut milk**
1 **Scotch bonnet chile**, left whole
1 tablespoon **thyme leaves**
1⅓ cups diced **potatoes**
1⅓ cups diced **carrots**
1½ cups **corn kernels** (either fresh, frozen, or canned)
2 **red bell peppers**, cored, seeded, and cut into ½ inch dice
**salt** and **pepper**
handful of chopped **fresh cilantro**, to garnish

**Heat** the oil in a saucepan and stir-fry the onion and garlic for 2–3 minutes.

**Increase** the heat, add the cayenne pepper, red lentils, stock, coconut milk, chile, thyme, potatoes, and carrots. Bring to a boil and simmer for 15–20 minutes.

**Season** and add the corn and bell pepper for the last 3 minutes of cooking.

**Remove** the Scotch bonnet chile, ladle the chowder into bowls and serve garnished with chopped cilantro and sprinkled with freshly ground black pepper.

**For corn & red pepper curry**, heat 1 tablespoon olive oil in a saucepan and fry 1 chopped onion and 2 chopped garlic cloves with 2½ cups corn kernels and 2 cored, seeded, and finely diced red bell peppers for 1–2 minutes. Add 1 tablespoon mild curry powder and 2½ cups coconut milk and bring to a boil. Cook for 3–4 minutes, remove from the heat and stir in ¼ cup finely chopped fresh cilantro before serving over ready-cooked rice. **Total cooking time 10 minutes.**

# desserts

# vanilla zabaglione

Serves **4**
Total cooking time **10 minutes**

6 **egg yolks**
¼ cup **sugar**
1 **vanilla bean**
¼ cup **marsala** or **dessert wine**
**biscotti**, to serve

**Place** the egg yolks and sugar in a heatproof bowl. Split the vanilla bean lengthwise, scrape out the seeds, add to the bowl and whisk together. Place the bowl over a saucepan of gently simmering water, taking care that the bottom of the bowl does not touch the water.

**Add** the marsala and whisk continuously with a hand-held electric mixer for 5–8 minutes, until the mixture is frothy and thickened. It should leave a trail when you remove the beaters. Pour into glass serving bowls and serve with biscotti.

**For vanilla egg nog**, bring 2 cups milk and ¾ cup light cream to a boil in a heavy saucepan with 1 split vanilla bean. Beat 4 egg yolks with ⅓ cup sugar in a heatproof bowl to combine, then slowly pour on the hot milk, stirring continuously. Return to the pan and cook over low heat for 5–10 minutes, until thickened. Place 4 oz chopped white chocolate in the heatproof bowl with 2 tablespoons brandy, if desired. Pour over the warm, thickened milk and stir until combined and the chocolate melted. Spoon into cups to serve. **Total cooking time 20 minutes.**

# tropical fruit salad

Serves **4**

Total cooking time **20 minutes**

2 **lemon grass stalks**,
coarsely chopped

²⁄₃ cup **water**

¾ cup **sugar**

½ cup sliced **pineapple**

1 **mango**, peeled and sliced

½ **papaya**, peeled and
chopped

**coconut macaroons** or
**coconut ice cream**, to serve

**Place** the lemon grass, measured water, and sugar in a small, heavy saucepan, bring to a boil and cook for 1 minute. Let cool slightly, then transfer to the freezer until completely cool, about 10 minutes.

**Arrange** the fruit in a serving bowl. Strain the syrup over the fruit and serve with macaroons or coconut ice cream, if desired.

**For sticky coconut rice with tropical fruit**, cook 1 cup short-grain pudding rice in a large saucepan of boiling water according to the package instructions. Transfer to a colander to drain. Add ½ cup coconut cream, 3 tablespoons sugar, and 1 lemon grass stalk to the pan and heat through. Return the rice to the pan, stir well and set aside for 10 minutes to cool. Peel and cut 1 mango and ½ pineapple into thin slices and serve with the coconut rice, topped with a sprinkling of shredded coconut. **Total cooking time 30 minutes.**

# rhubarb & ginger slump

Serves **4–6**

Total cooking time **30 minutes**

1½ lb **rhubarb**, trimmed and cut into chunks

1 tablespoon **flour**

¼ cup **granulated sugar**

2 pieces of **stem ginger in syrup**, drained and chopped, plus 2 tablespoons **syrup from the jar**

**Topping**

¾ cup **all-purpose flour**

¾ teaspoon **baking powder**

5 tablespoons **butter**, softened

5 tablespoons **granulated sugar**

¼ cup **milk**

1 **egg**, beaten

**Place** the rhubarb, flour, sugar, chopped ginger, and syrup in a shallow ovenproof dish and toss together. Cover with foil and place in a preheated oven, 375°F, for 3 minutes.

**Meanwhile,** place the ingredients for the topping in a food processor and blend until smooth. Uncover the rhubarb and spoon over the topping.

**Return** to the oven for another 25 minutes or until the topping is golden and cooked through.

**For rhubarb & ginger fools,** whip ¾ cup heavy cream until soft peaks form, then stir in 1 tablespoon confectioners' sugar. Gently stir in ½ cup drained and chopped canned rhubarb and divide among serving bowls. Crumble 1 ginger cookie over each portion and serve immediately. **Total cooking time 10 minutes.**

# chocolate fondue

Serves **4**

Total cooking time **10 minutes**

1¼ cups **heavy cream**
2 tablespoons **orange liqueur**
    (optional)
5 oz **dark chocolate**, chopped
5 oz **milk chocolate**, chopped

**To serve**
**marshmallows**
**cookies**
**mini doughnuts**

**Bring** the cream to a boil in a small, heavy saucepan. Remove from the heat and stir in the liqueur, if using, and the chocolate until melted. Transfer to a warmed serving bowl or fondue pot, if desired.

**Arrange** the marshmallows, cookies, and mini doughnuts on a serving plate, spear them on long forks and dip them into the warm chocolate.

**For chocolate & marshmallow trifle**, place 2 cups mini marshmallows, 3½ tablespoons butter, and 2 cups chopped chocolate in a heavy saucepan and melt over low heat until smooth. Stand the pan in a bowl of cold water and let cool for 5–10 minutes. Whip 1 cup heavy cream until it holds its shape, then stir in 1 teaspoon vanilla extract and the cooled chocolate mixture. Arrange bite-size chunks of plain cake in the bottom of a serving dish and spoon the chocolate mixture on top. Sprinkle with a handful of raspberries and blueberries to serve. **Total cooking time 20 minutes.**

# apple & orange tart

Serves **4**
Total cooking time **30 minutes**

1 sheet **store-bought puff pastry**
5 **dessert apples**, cored and thinly sliced
6 tablespoons **sugar**
finely grated zest of 1 **orange**

**Place** the pastry on a baking sheet and use a sharp knife to lightly score a ½ inch border around the edges, taking care not to cut right through the pastry. Prick all over the center of the pastry with a fork.

**Toss** the apples with 5 tablespoons of the sugar and the orange zest, then arrange on top of the pastry. Sprinkle with the remaining sugar. Place in a preheated oven, 425°F, for 20 minutes, until the apples are tender and the pastry is crisp.

**For apple & orange brioche tarts**, cut out a circle from each of 4 slices of brioche, using a cup as a guide. Butter both sides and arrange on a baking sheet. Mix ¼ cup ground almonds and ¼ cup sugar with 3 tablespoons mascarpone cheese and the finely grated zest of ½ orange, then spoon onto the brioche. Arrange 2 cored and thinly sliced apples on top, then sprinkle with 2 tablespoons sugar. Place in a preheated oven, 400°F, for 15–20 minutes, until golden. **Total cooking time 20 minutes.**

# strawberry cream puffs

Serves **4**
Total cooking time **20 minutes**

1 sheet **store-bought puff pastry**
¼ cup **confectioners' sugar**
1¼ cups **heavy cream**
2 cups **strawberries**, hulled and halved

**Cut** the pastry into 12 equal rectangles and arrange on a baking sheet. Place another baking sheet on top to prevent the pastry from puffing up too much during cooking. Place in a preheated oven, 400°F, for 10 minutes, until golden and crisp.

**Sift** half the confectioners' sugar over the pastry puffs and cook under a preheated hot broiler for 30 seconds, until the sugar melts. Let cool.

**Whip** the cream with the remaining confectioners' sugar until soft peaks form. Arrange the pastry strips, whipped cream, and strawberries on plates and serve immediately.

**For strawberry cream pots**, whip 1¼ cups heavy cream with ½ teaspoon vanilla extract and 2 tablespoons confectioners' sugar until soft peaks form. Stir in 1 cup hulled and chopped strawberries and divide among small glass bowls. Serve with shortbread cookies. **Total cooking time 10 minutes.**

# apricot & almond crostata

Serves **6–8**

Total cooking time **30 minutes**

**butter**, for greasing

**confectioners' sugar**, for
  dusting

8 oz **pie crust**

5 oz **marzipan**, sliced

8 **apricots**, halved and pitted

¼ cup sliced **almonds**

2 tablespoons **milk**

2 tablespoons **sugar**

**Lightly** grease a baking sheet. Dust a work surface with confectioners' sugar, then roll out the pastry into a 14 inch circle. Place on the baking sheet, arrange the marzipan slices in the middle and top with the halved apricots.

**Sprinkle** the almonds over the top, then fold the edges of the pastry up and over to form a rough border. Brush the pastry border with the milk and sprinkle with the sugar.

**Place** in a preheated oven, 400°F, for 25 minutes, until the pastry is just cooked through. Serve with cream or custard, if desired.

**For baked apricots stuffed with almonds**, place 4 oz amaretti cookies in a food processor with 3 tablespoons blanched almonds, 1 egg white, and 2 tablespoons sugar and pulse to form a rough paste. Halve 9 apricots, and arrange cut sides up in a shallow ovenproof dish, then place a little of the almond mixture on top of each apricot. Place in a preheated oven, 400°F, for 10–15 minutes, until the fruit is tender and the topping is crisp. **Total cooking time 20 minutes.**

# cinnamon-spiced cherries

Serves **4**
Total cooking time **10 minutes**

2 tablespoons **sugar**
1½ cups **rosé wine**
strip of pared **lemon** peel
1 **cinnamon stick**
1 lb **cherries**, pitted

**Combine** all the ingredients in a saucepan. Bring to a boil, then reduce the heat and simmer for 5 minutes, until the sugar has dissolved and the cherries are tender.

**Use** a slotted spoon to transfer the cherries to a serving dish, then cook the liquid over high heat for 3–4 minutes, until syrupy. Remove the cinnamon and lemon peel, then pour over the cherries and serve warm or cold.

**For cherry & cinnamon soup**, heat 1¾ cups fruity white wine in a saucepan with ⅓ cup sugar, 1 cinnamon stick, 1 strip of pared orange peel, and a good squeeze of orange juice. Simmer for 10 minutes, then add 1 lb pitted cherries and cook for 5 minutes, until tender. Remove the orange peel and cinnamon, add ⅔ cup mascarpone cheese and puree with an immersion blender until smooth. Add a few ice cubes to cool the soup, then spoon into serving bowls and sprinkle with chocolate shavings and a few more pitted cherries. **Total cooking time 20 minutes.**

# chocolate fudge brownie

Serves **8**
Total cooking time **30 minutes**

1¾ sticks **butter**
7 oz **dark chocolate**, chopped
¾ cup **firmly packed dark
  brown sugar**
¾ cup **granulated sugar**
4 **eggs**, beaten
½ cup **ground almonds**
⅔ cup **all-purpose flour**
**vanilla ice cream**, to serve
  (optional)

**Melt** the butter and chocolate over low heat in a shallow ovenproof dish, about 9 inches across. Remove from the heat and cool for a couple of minutes.

**Beat** together the sugars and eggs, then stir in the chocolate mixture followed by the almonds and flour.

**Wipe** the rim of the ovenproof dish with a damp piece of paper towel to neaten, then pour in the mixture. Place in a preheated oven, 350°F, for 25 minutes, until just set.

**Serve** warm with vanilla ice cream, if desired.

**For malted brownie sundaes**, bring ⅔ cup heavy cream to a boil in a small, heavy saucepan. Remove from the heat and stir in ½ cup chopped dark chocolate until smooth. Cut 7 oz ready-made brownies into small squares and place in the bottom of sundae glasses. Add 2 scoops of vanilla ice cream to each glass, then drizzle over the chocolate sauce. Coarsely crush 2 oz malted chocolate candies and sprinkle over the top to serve. **Total cooking time 10 minutes.**

# syrup sponge pudding

Serves **6**

Total cooking time **20 minutes**

1 ½ sticks **butter**, softened,
   plus extra for greasing

¾ cup **sugar**

1 ⅓ cups **all-purpose flour**

2 teaspoons **baking powder**

3 **eggs**

1 teaspoon **vanilla extract**

3 tablespoons **milk**

finely grated zest of ½ **lemon**

6 tablespoons **light corn
   syrup**

**cream** or **custard**, to serve

**Grease** a 5 cup pudding basin. Place all the ingredients, except the corn syrup, in a food processor and blend until smooth. Spoon ¼ cup of the corn syrup into the bottom of the basin, then add the pudding batter and smooth the surface with a knife.

**Cover** with microwave-proof plastic wrap and pierce the wrap a couple of times with a sharp knife. Cook in a microwave oven on medium heat for about 12 minutes. Test to see if it is cooked by inserting a toothpick into the pudding; it should come out clean.

**Let** rest for 3 minutes, then turn out onto a deep plate and spoon over the remaining corn syrup. Serve with cream or custard.

**For syrup-topped hotcakes**, place 1 ½ cups all-purpose flour in a food processor with 2 ½ teaspoons baking powder, 2 eggs, 1 cup milk, and a pinch of salt and blend until smooth. Heat a large, nonstick skillet. Add a little butter and swirl around the pan, then add generous tablespoonfuls of the batter. Cook for 2 minutes, until starting to set, then turn over and cook for another 1 minute. Remove from the pan, keep warm and repeat with the remaining batter. Serve the cakes sprinkled with blueberries and drizzled generously with light corn syrup. **Total cooking time 10 minutes.**

# lemon syllabub

Serves **4**
Total cooking time **10 minutes**

1¼ cups **heavy cream**
5 tablespoons **sweet white wine**
¼ cup **superfine sugar**
finely grated zest and juice of ½ **lemon**

**Whip** the cream until it just starts to hold its shape. Add the wine, one-third at a time, whipping well between each addition.

**Stir** in the sugar and lemon juice and continue whipping until fluffy and thick. Spoon into glasses, sprinkle with lemon zest and serve.

**For little lemon puddings**, beat 3½ tablespoons butter and ⅓ cup sugar with the finely grated zest of 1 lemon until light and fluffy. Add 2 egg yolks and ¼ cup lemon juice. Stir in 1 tablespoon flour, then 6 tablespoons heavy cream and ⅔ cup milk until smooth. Pour into 4 lightly greased 1 cup ramekins. Place the ramekins in a shallow roasting pan and pour boiling water into the pan until it comes halfway up the ramekins. Place in a preheated oven, 350°F, for 20–25 minutes, until golden and slightly risen. **Total cooking time 30 minutes.**

# prune clafoutis

Serves **4**

Total cooking time **30 minutes**

**butter**, for greasing

3 **eggs**

⅔ cup **sugar**

6 tablespoons **all-purpose flour**

⅔ cup **heavy cream**

⅔ cup **milk**

1 teaspoon **vanilla extract**

½ cup **pitted soft prunes**

**Lightly** grease a shallow ovenproof dish. Beat together the eggs and sugar until pale, frothy, and tripled in volume. Sift the flour into the bowl and lightly fold in. Add the cream, milk, and vanilla extract and mix until just combined.

**Pour** into the ovenproof dish and place in a preheated oven, 375°F, for 5 minutes, until the surface is just starting to set. Sprinkle with the prunes, then return to the oven for another 15–20 minutes, until the clafoutis is risen and golden.

**For plum crisp**, halve and pit 7 oz plums and place in a lightly greased ovenproof dish. Cut 2 tablespoons butter into small pieces and sprinkle over the plums with 2 tablespoons sugar. Cover with foil and place in a preheated oven, 400°F, for 10 minutes. Meanwhile, crush 4 oz ginger cookies and mix with 2 tablespoons softened butter. Remove the foil and sprinkle the cookie mixture over the plums. Return to the oven for another 5 minutes, until lightly crisp. **Total cooking time 20 minutes.**

# crunchy berry brûlée

Serves **4**
Total cooking time **20 minutes**

1 cup **mascarpone cheese**
1¼ cups **ready-made fresh custard**
1 cup **mixed berries**
½ cup **sugar**
1½ tablespoons **water**

**Beat** the mascarpone until smooth, then gently stir in the custard and transfer the mixture to a serving dish. Sprinkle the berries on top.

**Place** the sugar and measured water in a small, heavy saucepan and slowly bring to a boil, carefully swirling the pan from time to time. Keep cooking until the sugar dissolves, then turns a deep caramel color. Pour over the berries and leave for a few minutes to harden.

**For melting berry yogurt**, place 1¼ cups mixed berries in a serving dish. Spoon over 1¼ cups plain yogurt, then sprinkle with ⅓ cup firmly packed dark brown sugar. Chill in the refrigerator for 20–25 minutes, until the sugar has melted. **Total cooking time 30 minutes.**

# passion fruit & mango mess

Serves **4**
Total cooking time **10 minutes**

1 ¼ cups **heavy cream**
2–3 tablespoons
   **confectioners' sugar**
4 **meringue nests**, crushed
1 **mango**, peeled and sliced
1 **passion fruit**, halved

**Whip** the cream with the confectioners' sugar until it just holds its shape.

**Gently** stir in the meringue, most of the mango, and a little of the passion fruit pulp.

**Spoon** into glasses and top with the remaining fruit.

**For passion fruit & mango cream**, peel and chop 1 mango and divide among 4 glasses. Beat 1 egg yolk with 2 tablespoons superfine sugar until very frothy and pale, then stir in the pulp of 2 passion fruit. Whip ¾ cup heavy cream until soft peaks form, then stir into the egg mixture and whip until thickened. Add 1 tablespoon orange liqueur and 3 oz crushed meringues. Spoon over the mango and top with a little more chopped fruit, if desired. **Total cooking time 20 minutes.**

# index

# acknowledgments

**Commissioning editor:** Eleanor Maxfield
**Editor:** Polly Poulter
**Designer:** Tracy Killick
**Production controller:** Allison Gonsalves
**Americanizer:** Nicole Foster

**Photography:** Octopus Publishing Group Limited: Stephen
Conroy 7 right, 63, 75, 100-101, 105, 119, 137, 152-153,
161, 185, 195, 197, 204-205; Will Heap 6, 7 left, 8, 9 right,
19, 27, 41, 65, 67, 77, 79, 87, 95, 97, 111, 117, 123, 125,
127, 129, 131, 135, 149, 151, 155, 159, 163, 165, 171,
175, 179, 181, 187, 189, 191, 193, 199, 203; David Munns
10-11; Lis Parsons 1, 13, 17, 23, 29, 31, 33, 39, 43, 45, 47,
49, 59, 60-61, 69, 83, 93, 133, 139, 143, 145, 147, 167,
177, 183, 201; William Shaw 2, 4, 9 left, 15, 21, 25, 35, 37,
51, 53, 55, 57, 71, 73, 81, 85, 89, 91, 99, 103, 107, 109, 113,
115, 121, 141, 157, 169, 173, 207, 209, 211, 213, 215, 217,
219, 221, 223, 225, 227, 229, 231, 233.